A SAVIOUR OF LIVING CARGOES

After an earlier career as a Personal Assistant and raising a family, Carole returned to further education, studying for a B.A. in English Literature at Loughborough University, and a Masters Degree in Victorian Studies at Leicester University.

Whilst working on her dissertation for her Masters Degree, Carole came across the work of Caroline Chisholm and was hooked, successfully completing a Doctorate on Caroline's life and work several years later.

Carole believes that Caroline Chisholm deserves to be better known in Britain and hopes that this book will fill that gap expanding the knowledge of Caroline's life and work. She also hopes that the book will further raise Caroline's profile in Australia.

A SAVIOUR OF LIVING CARGOES

The Life and Work of Caroline Chisholm

Carole Walker

Wolds Publishing Limited

First published in Australia in 2009
Australian Scholarly Publishing Pty Ltd
7 Lt Lothian St Nth, North Melbourne, Vic 3051
TEL: 03 9329 6963 FAX: 03 9329 5452
EMAIL: aspic@ozemail.com.au
WEB: scholarly.info

First published in the UK in 2010
Wolds Publishing Limited
203 Six Hills Road, Walton on the Wolds, Leics LE12 8JF.
EMAIL: books@woldspublishing.co.uk
WEB: woldspublishing.co.uk

ISBN 978-0-9564724-0-3

Copyediting by Rhiannon Hart
Design and typesetting by Sarah Anderson
Printing and binding by gpex, Gerrards Cross, Bucks. www.gpex.co.uk
Cover lithograph by Thomas Fairland. Angelo Collen Hayter portrait of Caroline Chisholm. Courtesy of the National Library of Australia. (Accession number PIC U6413 NK4885)

CONTENTS

LIST OF ILLUSTRATIONS

ACKNOWLEDGEMENTS

I would like to thank all those archivists and librarians in all three continents who have given me so much help in pursuing documentation on Caroline Chisholm. The list is lengthy, but I include their names here, for without their help and advice this book would not have been possible. I apologise if I have inadvertently omitted names or organisations from the list, but that does not diminish my appreciation of their help.

Britain: The Archives of the Bishop of Birmingham; British Library – Newspaper Library, Colindale; The Oriental and India Office Collections and the Manuscript Department; Cathedral of Our Lady and St. Philip Howard, Arundel, West Sussex; The Catholic Record Society; Clan Chisholm Society, Scotland; Coutts & Company; Durham University Library; Professor M. H. Kaufman, and the Special Collections Section of the University Library, University of Edinburgh; Fawcett Library, Guildhall University; Fortrose Academy; Glasgow City Library; Greater London Record Office and Library; Highland Regional Archives; Inverness Library; Institute of Commonwealth Studies; The psychologist James Oliver; Leicester University Library; Lincolnshire Archives; The Sidney

Jones Library, Liverpool University; London Phrenology Company Limited; Loughborough University Library; Mary Evans Picture Library; Metropolitan Cathedral of St. George, Westminster; National Library of Scotland; Newcastle upon Tyne City Library; Margaret Osbourne and the staff of the Catholic Cathedral, Northampton; Oscott College, Sutton Coldfield; Our Lady's Presbytery, Olney, Buckingham; Records Office, Kew; Royal College of Physicians of Edinburgh; Royal Commonwealth Society Library; Royal Commission on Historical Manuscripts; The archives of the Bishop of Arundel & Brighton, St. Joseph's Hall, Sussex; Scottish Catholic Archives; The archives of The Rt. Hon. The Earl of Shaftesbury; David Weller, Senior Lecturer in American Politics, Nene College, Northampton; Trinity College Library, Cambridge; Warwickshire County Council Record Office; Warwickshire County Library; City of Westminster Archives; Westminster Diocesan Archives; Wigston Records Office, Leicestershire; Dr. Willimans's Library, London and the Archives of the Earl of Pembroke, Wiltshire Records Office.

Ireland: Cobh – Queenstown Story, Co. Cork; Cork Archives Institute; Cork City Library; Cork Public Museum; Limerick Regional Archives; Stokestown Famine Museum. My thanks also to Professor David Fitzpatrick and Simon J. Potter, History Department, Trinity College, Dublin and Professor Mary Daly, Professor of Modern History, University College, Dublin. Especial thanks to Felix Larkin for all his help and support.

Australia: The Australian Catholic University Library; Australian High Commission, London; Dr. R. Haines, Australian Research Council Fellow, Flinders University; Dr. Richard Reid, Australian War Memorial,

Canberra; Catholic Archdiocese of Sydney; Immigration Museum, Melbourne; Melbourne Diocesan Historical Commission; Melbourne University History Department; National Library of Australia, Canberra; John Moran at Preferential Publications; Royal Australian Historical Society; The Mitchell Library, State Library of New South Wales; State Library of Victoria, Melbourne; and Windsor Museum. I would also like to thank Audrey Carpenter, Doreen Robinson, Helen Buck and Joy and Barrie Atkinson who visited Australia on business and pleasure, and who, without much bullying, offered to do research and find particular books for me whilst in Australia.

India: My thanks to the Archivists at the Archives in Madras and Bombay.

Italy: My thanks to His Excellency Archbishop Luigi Barbarito, and Monsignor Charles Burns, Archivist at the Vatican, and his Excellency Monsignor Dino Monduzzi, Prefetto della Casa Pontificia.

I would particularly like to thank the staff at Northamptonshire Record Office, and Colin Eaton at Northampton Central Library for their invaluable help. My thanks too to the Northamptonshire local historians who have taken an interest in my research – especially Marcelle Grant, Raymond Gray and John Rigby, and the many members of the Northamptonshire Family History Society and Northamptonshire Record Society. Thanks also go to Brenda Stevens-Chambers for her help on Caroline's stay in Kyneton and to Rodney Stintson for his very helpful advice and support. My thanks to Miss Alison Maddock for her determination and perseverance at the Liverpool Record Office and Library; to Mike Rumbold, of the Weedon Bec History Society and Professor Holmes and Dr. Heathcote for their help on military matters. My thanks also go to Vada Hart of the Local Studies Department of Islington Central Reference Library who was always cheerful and very helpful.

My sincere thanks to Don and Judy Chisholm in Sydney. It was a delight and real pleasure to meet them, and to have the opportunity to discuss various aspects of Caroline's life with them, as well as see and touch the Chisholm memorabilia they have in their home.

It goes without saying that the support of my husband, Peter, and that of my two daughters, Susan and Dianah and her husband Ian has been of tremendous help. The support of my close friends, particularly Ann Pull, Janet Procter-Blain, Dorothy and Ray Hardie has been of immense help to me in keeping me on the straight and narrow. It is a great sadness that Ann and Ray, who helped me through difficulties and problems, successes and failures, ill health and flood, are not here to see the completed book. My particular thanks too to Mike Pickering, who supervised my doctorate thesis on Caroline Chisholm at Loughborough University. His help was invaluable.

My sincere thanks also go to Lyn Hedges for her help with the UK edition of the book, and to Elliot Banks of gpex for his help and advice in preparing and printing the UK edition of the biography.

And last, but by no means least, to my dear friend Bev Adam in Perth, Australia, who initially stirred my interest in nineteenth century emigration that subsequently led to my studies of Caroline Chisholm.

PREFACE

The British reader who picks up this book will be thinking 'Caroline who?', while the Australian will probably know of Caroline Chisholm but not be entirely sure of what she did. The purpose of this biography is to bring Caroline to a wider audience in Australia and to the attention of a readership in Britain, where her significant work in helping others has been largely forgotten. That work was a lifetime spent in helping poor emigrants to Australia, both on their arrival and their journey out, which had the consequential effect of improving conditions on board ship for all who were emigrating from Britain.

Caroline's father, William Jones, died when Caroline was only six. He was the son of an agricultural labourer and he had worked hard to improve his living standards, and was able to leave his wife comfortably off and properties to several of his children. Caroline's marriage to Archibald Chisholm gave her the opportunity to travel abroad, but her means were limited and marriage did not bring with it financial security. To the contrary, the family were often in dire financial straits, and her work was subsidised by Archibald's wage and pension from the East India Company army and by monies raised by friends and supporters. Caroline would not take funds from any religious or governmental body or organisation as she felt this would curtail her independence. What she did was therefore all the more significant. Unlike a Florence Nightingale or Elizabeth Fry, she did not have the wealth and the influence that that wealth brings.

That Caroline was as well known as Florence Nightingale in the mid-nineteenth century is difficult to believe today. A number of poems were, however, written to sing her praises, and the artist Angelo Collen Hayter exhibited a portrait of her at the Royal Academy in London in 1852. Many articles about her were published in *The Times*, the *Illustrated London News*, *Household Words*, Douglas Jerrold's *Weekly Newspaper*, the *Sydney Morning Herald*, *The Argus*, the *Empire*, *Chambers' Edinburgh Journal*, *The Lady's Newspaper* and other periodicals. The following extracts from newspapers of the time give a better understanding of just how well known and how popular she was:

> Among the practical benefactors of our emigrant countrymen stands pre-eminent Mrs Chisholm, whose efforts in their behalf have been not more remarkable for their success than for the gentle yet persevering wisdom with which they have been pursued.
>
> — *Chambers' Edinburgh Journal*, 30 March 1850

> The Chairman, His Worship the Mayor, rose and said that the present was an occasion which seldom offered itself to the citizens of Cork. They had at their table that night a lady whose benevolence, charity and great amiability of disposition were so well known to the whole world, there was little left for him to say on the subject.
>
> — 'A Soirée for Mrs Chisholm before the ship Peru left Cork', *The Cork Examiner*, 12 May 1852

Mrs Chisholm ... had acquired fame and honour by the energy with which she had devoted herself to the amelioration of the condition of the emigrants and also of the convicts. She had exhibited the most indomitable courage ... and the meeting would evince their respect for that great and glorious woman.

— 'Report of Meeting, Testimonial to Mrs Chisholm in front of an audience of eminent bankers and merchants of the City of London', *The Times*, 10 August 1853

Caroline's work spanned three continents: Europe, Asia and Australia. She worked tirelessly for the betterment of conditions for emigrants and, particularly initially, single women leaving Britain to settle in the colonies of Australia. That she and her great achievements have been largely forgotten, especially in Britain, is unfortunate.

There are several biographies of Caroline Chisholm. The earlier works were written in Victorian times, and were written in the Victorian eulogistic style. A few of the later biographies were written with the beatification of Caroline in mind, and it is difficult to see the woman behind the image. My aim has been to understand the factors that motivated Caroline.

Unlike the earlier biographies, this book gives details of Caroline's upbringing. It also places her within the context of nineteenth century British history, as we now see it.

Research in archives in the UK, India and Australia and recent secondary sources has added to our knowledge of this remarkable woman.

The number of emigrants who sailed under the auspices of the Family Colonisation Loan Society was small when compared to the total numbers who emigrated to Australia, but the improvements that Caroline insisted upon for the emigrants on board the Society ships set an example for other shipowners to follow, however reluctantly. This led to improvements in the Passenger Acts and helped many to endure the journey to Australia, America, Canada, New Zealand or South Africa. Caroline effectively publicised the difficulties faced by emigrants and their families, and showed that much could be done by means of careful planning and practical schemes to alleviate distress and foster re-settlement abroad. Percival Serle, writing in his biography of Caroline Chisholm for the *Dictionary of Australian Biography* in 1949, wrote that 'no greater woman has been connected with Australia'.

A saucer depicting Caroline, believed to have been presented to her by friends in Wales.
By kind permission of Don Chisholm.

INTRODUCTION

Biographers take their subject's life in their hands. They gather material from a number of sources and sift it to find what is relevant, influenced by many different factors and concerns.

The task of writing a new biography of Caroline Chisholm is made difficult by a number of misconceptions in early biographies. The reiteration, over time, has created a number of Caroline Chisholms. She has been portrayed as a saintly woman, a role model that the Roman Catholic Church could hold up for laywomen to follow. It has been claimed that the Catholic Church has used Caroline as one of the proofs of its Australian, rather than Irish, roots.[1] There are claims that the reason for Caroline's fame has been a lack of research into upper- and middle-class women in the period before the gold rushes—that Caroline is seen as a lone pioneer rather than a late-comer to the philanthropic scene.[2] More recently Caroline has been marginalised as being anti-feminist for not actively supporting the fight for equal rights, and for placing single women in employment as servants in the interior of Australia where she knew bachelors were looking for wives. There is also the claim that Caroline's status was founded on the fact that she was a woman who moved into the male domain at a time when women were confined to the domestic realm. She has been called Australia's 'first social worker' and 'first minister for social security'. She has been praised for her confidence and determination but criticised for her apologetic nature, censured for neglecting her children and rebuked for ignoring the plight of the Aborigines.

These multiple views have contributed to a lack of historical acknowledgement, particularly in Britain. The present author agrees that Caroline was not alone in her efforts, but in the mid-nineteenth century, she fought for the education, health and welfare of others in a role which can best be described as that of a women's activist. She achieved much in spite of her lower-middle-class background and the restrictions that women in her time had to cope with.

There is a tension in the perception of Caroline as the heroic pioneer who accepted the displacement of Indigenous Australians. However, in a letter to Earl Grey Caroline commented upon the evils of the disparity of the sexes in Australia and saw the effect this was having on 'those unfortunate tribes, the Aborigines of New Holland'. She requested of Earl Grey 'the speedy and parental interference of a humane Government' to come to the aid of the Aborigines.[3] She was aware of, and understood, the problems caused by the displacement of Indigenous populations, and was not afraid to voice an unpopular opinion on such a subject.

Caroline was also aware that if Europeans went on humiliating and insulting the Chinese, there would be trouble. She showed her concern regarding Chinese immigration and the wider aspect of the equality of humankind, whatever their ethnic or religious background, when she wrote to the editor of *The Argus* in 1857:

there will be no rest until man is recognised as man, without distinction of colour or clime. All that labour requires from capital is a clear stage and no favour, and then the more wrestling the better for civilisation, education, and religion. The monopolising spirit of capital and power has locked up India, and would now shut the gates of China against the will of Providence and the rights of man; nevertheless the education of the labourer is going on. He begins to see, and to feel, and understand, the value of finger labour, and as this physical education advances, crowned heads will begin to repose in peace. They will then learn to settle their differences in some other way, for the rights and influence of labour will not be thoroughly understood or appreciated until a soldier's pay is five shillings a day. Thus free labour may become in time the universal peacemaker amongst mankind.[4]

It is true, though, that Caroline did not have her children with her at the Immigrants' Home in Sydney. Caroline wrote that it was her plan:

to have apartments near the office for my children, but this did not answer—at night I must be in the Home. I gave up one child, and thought I could keep two with me, but I found the elder a source of so much anxiety that I consented to part with him. I knew, under the honest care of Miss Galvin, of Windsor, they would be well fed and kindly treated, and I could still keep one, my youngest. Some sickness among the children in the tents told me plainly my duty. Still I would not, could not give him up. A lady, whose esteem I value, told me I could not, must not, risk my child's life; that I must either give up the Home, or my selfish feeling for my child. I was aware of the truth of her

> observation, but refused. At night, as was usual with me, I saw the girls, after they had retired to rest. Ninety-four were in that dwelling. I asked if they had any place to go to if I turned them out, not one had a place of shelter. On my return to the office, I found a poor woman waiting to ask for a white gown, to make her dead bairn [child] decent. I went into my room, packed up my little fellow's wardrobe, and the next day he was at Windsor. This was the last sacrifice it was God's will to demand.[5]

Caroline ensured that in following 'God's will' her children would be protected 'under the honest care of Miss Galvin, of Windsor', who would feed and 'kindly' treat them.

Caroline's letter to Bishop Ullathorne shows her concern for her children. (See page 114) She was aware of the consequences of 'following out of my vocation' and 'duty'. She writes of her sons: 'Archy is a great comfort to me … dear William, … dear Henry.' Archibald junior also assisted his mother in her work, as is noted in reports of her visit to Ireland. The boys flanked Caroline at a meeting before their sailing back to Australia in 1854. She resided with Archibald junior in Sydney after her husband returned to England in 1865 with their children Sydney, Caroline and Monica. Henry often visited his mother at his brother's home. Archibald junior escorted his mother back to England the following year. These are not actions of a family who felt themselves neglected.

To sift through the major biographies of Caroline is to reflect on the changing attitudes towards her and to biographical studies. It shows how Eneas Mackenzie's ambiguities and errors have been used and re-used by following biographers in creating myths about Caroline's place of birth and the time spent in Brighton, for instance. What also becomes apparent is that the last two biographies of Caroline have come full circle in their attitude towards her. Mackenzie and Samuel Sidney created the saint-like woman; the woman on the pedestal; the model of the angel in the house who moved into the public arena to care for the poor emigrants, as a mother would care for her children. This was a model to be emulated. Mary Hoban and Joanna Bogle's biographies carry overtones of the saintly woman. Hoban makes no secret of her wish that the Roman Catholic Church 'will raise [Caroline] to the position from which she can continue her good work'.[6] Bogle emphasises that Caroline's 'life has many useful messages for today—the championing of family values, common sense, practicality, the belief in human capacity to overcome problems and to achieve' and, particularly, her 'sincere, but never dogmatic religious beliefs'.[7]

I came across the work of Caroline Chisholm when I read *Single Female Emigration to Australia in the 19th Century* at Leicester University. Further research into this remarkable woman led to me completing a doctorate at Loughborough University on Caroline's life and work. I am a woman, towards the end of middle age, who does not attend church regularly but lives a Christian life. I believe that by stripping away some of the myths and religious and eulogistic views there will be a better understanding of the character of Caroline Chisholm and the motivations that lay behind her work in the field of emigration. By portraying Caroline in her ordinariness I hope I show Caroline's achievements for what they are, something quite extraordinary.

St. Sepulchre's Church

THE EARLY YEARS, 1808–1832

On 30 May 1808, 37-year-old Sarah Jones gave birth to a daughter, Caroline. Sarah had been twenty when she had married 47-year-old William Jones on 24 October 1791. During seventeen years of marriage she had had seven children, of whom Caroline was to be the last. Sarah could so easily have lost her life in childbirth, as two of William's previous three wives had done.

William's first child, James, had been born forty-six years earlier to his first wife, Elizabeth Pettit, on 8 May 1762. They weren't married at the time; William didn't marry Elizabeth until James was six months old, but to have a child outside wedlock was not unusual. It proved Elizabeth's fertility, and a poor family had to provide for itself.[1] By the time Caroline was born, William had come a long way from his humble beginnings and had much to be grateful for. Most members of his large family lived within close proximity to his home in the Mayorhold in Northampton.

William Jones had grown up in the village of Wootton, about two miles south of Northampton, before its enclosure in 1778/79. His father, John, was a farm labourer, and he and his wife, Mary, had four other sons and one daughter. Wootton was a typical Midland village, in which people lived within it and went out daily to tend the land. It was lucky enough not to have one dominating landowner who dictated to the rest of the community. The villagers themselves had control of the manorial rights, kept a tight reign on affairs and did not allow the village to become large and straggling.[2]

William showed considerable initiative and worked extremely hard to raise his living standard above that of his father. He moved with his young family to Duston to obtain work as a shoemaker.[3] After five years of marriage his wife died in giving birth to a daughter, named Elizabeth after her mother. For a further five years William lived in Duston with his three young children. In June 1772 he married for the second time. Five years later, William's second wife died, a month after the birth of her third child. Seven years later William married again. Following this marriage the family moved into the Mayorhold in Northampton, close to his new wife's family, who lived in the adjoining parish. William's third wife died in July 1789. It was three years after the death of his third wife that William married Caroline's mother, Sarah Allen (Allum/em), at the Church of the Holy Sepulchre in Northampton.

Northampton was a compact, thriving market town in an agricultural county. It was 'pleasantly situated' sixty-six miles from London on the 'thoroughfare road between London, Liverpool, and Manchester'. The opening of a branch canal in May 1815 between the River Nene and the Grand Junction enhanced the town's accessibility.[4] The town catered to the land-owning aristocracy with a theatre, regular balls, concerts, lectures and literary gatherings. The middle and professional classes and retailers were concerned with the social, religious, scientific and literary interests of the town. Regular markets were held including cattle markets, livestock and horse fairs. Not long after moving into the town, William abandoned shoemaking and became a victualler, or an innkeeper. Many victuallers at that time brewed their own beer.

William then turned his hand to pig rearing, and by the time Sarah gave birth to Caroline he was a well-established pig dealer. He owned 'a close, or inclosed ground … situate and being near Castle Hills' and 'gardens and outbuilding … situate in the Mayorhold'.[5] The Mayorhold was a working-class area in the parish of St Sepulchre's.[6] In later life, Caroline was to write of the pig as the 'poor man's friend', the 'comfort and hope to thousands', and ponder 'how many debts wait to be paid until the pig be killed?'; 'how many new dresses are bought with her bacon?'[7] Caroline may have been reflecting on her childhood.

Two anecdotes highlight the philanthropic predisposition of William Jones and are reported as 'the remote cause of instilling the ideas that ruled [Caroline's] life in after years'.[8] Eneas Mackenzie, Caroline's first biographer, wrote of the first incident:

> One day this high minded man [William Jones] introduced to his house a poor maimed soldier whom he attended with respect and affection, and calling his children pointed out what obligations they were under to this veteran; he having fought the enemies of England amid the perils of sea and land, and sacrificed his limbs, that they might live in ease, comfort and security at home. This old soldier excited the curiosity of the children by descriptions of other countries, the beauty of the scenery, the excellence of climate, the abundance of food, the advantages that would accrue by the possession of those paradises as colonies, and the fortunes emigrants might reap.[9]

In 1914, an essay by Edith Pearson related the following tale:

> Caroline's father one day at the midday meal heard a great commotion in the village, and went to see the cause. He found an old priest being followed by a great crowd of people, who were pelting him with stones and mud. He rebuked and dispersed the people, and brought the priest into his home and family. The old man was an honoured guest for many weeks, tended and supplied with food and clothes. During the time of his stay the priest and little Caroline became great companions. He had travelled much, and Caroline drank in all his lovely stories of foreign parts. On the day he left her father's home they had a celebration at the mid-day meal, when (as was the custom at that time) toasts were given and speeches made. We can hear the dear old priest, in his broken English, expressing his deep gratitude for all that had been done for him: he prayed to God to 'bless this home and especially this child' (little Caroline who was seated next to him), and Mrs Chisholm's daughter tells us that 'he laid his hand in blessing on his little friend's head'. Ever after the departure of the old priest his prayers and influence were over her.[10]

The similarity of the stories is problematical, and with the passage of time a single incident may have been split into two. Margaret Kiddle, writing a biography of Caroline in Australia in 1950, believed that the 'legendary' story that 'a refugee French priest, whom her father had befriended, first turned her thoughts towards Catholicism, had 'no basis in fact'.[11]

William Jones died on 4 April 1814 at the age of seventy and was buried at the Anglican Church of St Sepulchre's. His will shows how far he had come from his humble beginnings. He left Sarah £500 and several properties to his surviving twelve children. Many years later, in *Little Joe*, her novelette, Caroline, commenting on the death of Joe's mother, wrote that it was 'astonishing how at times early sorrow and adversity change and form the character of youth—the lively and playful stripling becomes all at once, under this character, the thoughtful man; and this was the case with Joe'.[12] The siblings nearest in age to Caroline when their father died would have been fourteen and ten; an age when they could well have been working, leaving Caroline, like Joe, with 'much earnest industry evinced to help' her.[13]

Plowman Jones, William's brother and executor of his will, shared characteristics with his deceased brother. He too showed considerable initiative and worked hard to raise his living standard. Plowman took advantage of the growing sheep-farming industry within Wootton parish and started his working life as a shepherd, but by the time he died in 1821 he was working as a lace manufacturer. Dealing in lace was quite profitable and Plowman's personal estate on his death in Wootton in 1821 was declared as being near £300. He bequeathed 'a yard, Garden Ground and appurtenances thereabouts' to his son, William, and other real estate cottages and closed land to his wife, Mary, which on her death was to be sold and divided between the other children.[14]

Caroline's half-brother William inherited his father's good business sense. He developed the pig-dealing trade and was able to leave a number of properties to his large family.

Little is known or can be traced of Caroline's mother, Sarah. She was born in 1771 and died in April 1859. Caroline had returned to Australia by then, and news of her mother's death would not have reached her until August 1859, at the very earliest. Thoughts of her mother would have been uppermost in her mind when she penned *Little Joe*, which was serialised in the *Empire* in Sydney in 1859–60. She wrote 'there was a peaceful calm, a domestic serenity in her acts that made Mrs Brown's countenance pleasing to look at. There is something very beautiful to contemplate in the face when the aspirations of a well-disposed mind in a manner illuminates the features, and leaves its own impression and the most striking beauty in the widow's face was the stamp of humanity; her face was an index of her pure and peaceful mind; her charity of thought and soundness of judgement were daily exercised; her children often heard her praise, but never censure; she was one of those made to love and to be loved.'[15] Significantly, when Caroline drew up the rules and regulations of the Female School of Industry for the Daughters of the European Soldiers she founded in Madras shortly after her arrival there in 1833, she wrote that the 'rod was to be spared and only used as a last resort'. Such words may well have been a recollection of her mother's maxim to praise and never censure her children.

It was in Samuel Sidney's *Emigrant's Journal*, published in August 1849, that the adult Caroline recalled her first attempts at colonisation[16] and gives us a rare glimpse of her childhood. She wrote of a game she:

> carried on in a wash-hand basin, before I was six years old. I made boats of broad beans, expended all my money in touchwood dolls—removed families—located them in the bed-quilt, and sent the bolts, filled with wheat, back to their friends, of which I kept a store in a thimble case. At length I upset the basin, which I judged to be a facsimile of the sea, spoilt a new bed, got punished, and afterwards carried out my plan in a dark cellar, with a rushlight stuck upon a tin-kettle; and, strange as it may seem, many of the ideas which I have since carried out, first gained possession of

> my mind at that period; and, singular as it may appear, I had a Wesleyan minister and a Catholic priest in the same boat. Two of my dolls were very refractory, and would not be obedient; this made me name them after two persons I knew who were constantly quarrelling, and I spent hours in listening to their supposed debates, to try and find out how I could manage them; at length I put the two into a boat, and told them if they were not careful they would be drowned; and having landed them *alive*, I knelt down to pray to God to make them love each other.

That Caroline 'knelt down to pray to God to make them love each other' gives us some idea of the importance of religion to her. The game also foreshadows her desire to work for the good of all, regardless of creed. As she wrote the passage she might well have noted the irony that even as a young girl she often spent all her pocket money on 'removing families'.

It would seem unlikely that Sarah Jones formally educated her children. She made her mark rather than sign either her marriage entry or her will. The pamphlets and letters that Caroline wrote in later life show however a well-educated, methodical and meticulous woman, and she obviously achieved a high standard of instruction. By the age of nine, as a witness at her sister Charlotte's wedding, Caroline was able to sign her name. Her education appears to be well above that of her siblings and half-siblings. Edith Pearson relates the incident of a burglar breaking into the home of an aged lady in Northampton with whom Caroline was living.[17] Caroline may have been sent to this lady to be educated by her. There were a number of academies in the town, three of which were for ladies.[18] In the main, schools in Northampton were associated with the various places of worship, including the Dissenter's College. From 1786 there were eleven Sunday Schools.[19] The

General Sunday School, which was not affiliated to any church, became redundant in 1823. The Lancastrian boys' school was founded in 1811 and the girls' school in 1815. Few records of the earlier schools exist, and regrettably no record can be found of Caroline's education.

As Caroline's father died in 1814 when she was only six, it is not unreasonable to suggest that it would have been her mother's influence that was paramount to her upbringing. Sarah was of the evangelical persuasion, and Caroline, in her lectures, emigration talks, papers and in *Little Joe*, often referred to the 'overflowing tenderness of the poor' and the 'duty the rich owed to the poor'.[20] Caroline also wrote 'he who gives from an overflowing purse comparatively gives but little to him who gives his mite from a scanty one'.[21] Such sentiments were very much part of the evangelical spiritual revival. Mackenzie wrote that 'as womanhood dawned, the poor became the object of her attention; the trivial vanities of teenhood were neglected in the performance of duties to her indigent neighbours; considering the fulfilment of Christ's ordinances beyond that of personal ease and selfish vanity, she appeared to live for the sake of others, entirely forgetful of self'.[22]

Caroline grew up in a period of transition and rapid industrialisation. At the time of her birth Britain had been at war with France for fifteen years, and it wasn't until she was six years old that the fighting ended. The various battles were reported in the *Northampton Mercury*, but the war, unless families had male relatives involved in the fighting, was of less consequence to the majority of people than the increased prices of bread and other foods that resulted from Napoleon's attempts to defeat Britain by attacking British trade. With high unemployment and low wages the increases were a disaster for the workers, and in 1810 there were food riots. During Caroline's early childhood the effects of the war and industrial developments displaced many manual workers. In the Midlands and in parts of Yorkshire the misery and poverty saw framework knitters and hand-loom weavers uniting to destroy the newly introduced textile machines. Caroline was seven in 1815 when accounts of the Peterloo riots and the furore that followed were widely reported in the press.

The people of Northampton would have felt the pinch of rising grain prices as sharply as they were felt elsewhere in Britain. For some industries, peace in 1815 brought a decline in trade with the fall in demand for goods for the army, but Northampton and the county generally suffered less than the southern counties. The town was cosseted by the shoemaking trade. It was the cheapness of labour that attracted the London wholesalers to put work out to Northampton, where children as young as six and seven were taught stabbing and stitching, with men doing the knife-work and tooling.[23] Social ills, such as the employment of young children, gave rise to radicalism within the town. Political reform would have been talked about in the small workshops, as would have been the reports in the local papers of the local corporation candidate at Northampton being paid £1,000 out of corporate funds for electoral purposes during the 1826 elections, and in February the following year.[24]

The working classes of Northampton formed the Working Men's Association and the Female Radical Association. Such organisations affiliated to become the Chartist movement, and their demands were universal suffrage, vote by ballot, equal representation, payment of members of parliament and no property qualification for voting, as well as the request to shorten the life of parliaments to five years.

The young Caroline would have been aware of what was happening in the town, and she most likely would have had a general knowledge of affairs of state, questions of social reform and conflicts between contending interests and values. As some members of the Jones family had radical tendencies, this is not unreasonable to suppose.[25] Throughout her working life Caroline strongly advised her audiences at emigration and political lectures to read the newspapers, advice that she herself followed. Towards the end of her life in Australia in 1859/60, Caroline gave four political lectures in support of the Chartist cause.

When Caroline was in her early twenties, she met Archibald Chisholm. Ten years older than Caroline, he was born on 15 February 1798 at Knockfin in the parish of Kilmorack, Inverness-shire. He was the son of John Chisholm, a farmer, and his first wife, Jean (née Fraser, of Culbokie). John, as one of the principal cadets, or heirs, of the Chisholm Clan, would have leased the land from the Laird, Colin of Knockfin.[26] Archibald's father married twice—there were four sons from the first marriage, of whom Archibald was the youngest, and two sons from the second, to Hannah Fraser of Achnaloich. The family had a long tradition of Roman Catholicism. Archibald's half-brother Thomas (1807–72) was a priest in Strathglass, and close cousins included Bishop John Chisholm (1752–1814) and Bishop Eneas Chisholm (1759–1818).[27]

Like many of his clansmen, Archibald knew Gaelic as well as English. He was educated at Fortrose Academy, founded in 1791, but sadly its records do not go back far enough to tell us of Archibald's attainments. We do know from his application form for his entry into the East India Company's Army in 1818 that he had a 'classical' education. As there was no provision for boarders at the time of Archibald's attendance at Fortrose, and as the family home was about thirty-five miles away, Archibald would most likely have lived with relatives on his mother's side on the Black Isle. There was an element of fee-paying to provide for teachers' salaries, but free tuition was available to some students whose parents could not afford to pay. This is in line with Scottish education of the period, which was far more advanced than it was in England. Among the academy's objectives today, and not far removed from those in the early 1800s, is to develop pupils' talents to encourage the highest possible level of academic attainment, and to foster an atmosphere of diligence, tolerance, co-operation and mutual respect at all times.

Archibald followed in the footsteps of his brothers John and William when he joined the East India Company army.[28] Both parents had died and his uncle William Fraser certified Archibald's parentage on 12 May 1818 for his nomination as a cadet for the Madras Establishment. It was on 28 May that Charles Grant, a director of the company, having enquired into Archibald's character, connections and qualifications, certified that he had found Archibald to be a fit person. Archibald was duly appointed as an ensign in June 1818 and arrived in Madras on 29 September that year. He was posted to the 15th Native Infantry Regiment and was based at Fort St George in Madras.[29] Only a month later, Archibald was made a lieutenant of the 15th regiment.

Fort St George had been built in 1640 and many officers lived within its walls. It was also known as White Town for the colour of its buildings, and covered a square mile. It contained dwellings, shops and taverns, as well as the barracks.[30] The city itself had some fine buildings. However, in 1837 a young ensign, Cumming, wrote 'Madras has quite disappointed my expectations. There are only one or two good houses in the place, the rest are small shabby houses inhabited by poor people.'[31] Cumming would also have been unimpressed by the verminous soldiers' barracks, the poor hygiene and unsanitary conditions, and would have understood why the men preferred sleeping in the street, except in the monsoon season.[32]

The officers wore high-necked, gold-buttoned red tunics with epaulettes. There was a sword shoulder strap with a buckle, on which was engraved M.N.I. XV (Madras Native Infantry, 15th Regiment). The men wore scarlet tunics, white pantaloons and a black headdress. In such clothes, in the heat of India, it is not surprising that the lives of serving officers and civilians were hampered by ill health, as indeed Archibald's health suffered. Even off duty, attending official balls and dances, such apparel would have been obligatory.

The 15th Native Infantry became the 30th Regiment in 1824. In June that year Archibald took on the duties of quartermaster and paymaster to his corps. As quartermaster Archibald was not only responsible for provisions and the accommodation for the regiment, but also for collecting and examining the regimental abstracts and attending to the pay of the men.[33]

Archibald had taken leave in India and had portions cancelled in June 1824 to fight in the Opium Wars. He was granted a furlough on 22 January 1828 and sailed for England on 24 February on the *Marquis of Wellington* with thirty other passengers. After ten years' service he was entitled to two years' leave.

Previous biographers have suggested that Archibald went to Northampton upon arrival in England because he was based at the barracks there or at Weeden Bec. However, these were British Army barracks and as such were not for the use of members of the East India Company army. In fact, it was only as a courtesy that officers of the company were allowed to use their titles outside company territories. Archibald could have been travelling from London to Scotland to visit family relatives and have broken his journey in Northampton, or been in the town for the hunting. Whatever the reason for his being in Northampton, it was there that he met Caroline.

Archibald proposed marriage to 22-year-old Caroline Jones towards the end of 1830. Mackenzie informs us that at a public meeting 'Mrs Chisholm related … that her strong faith in having a divine mission to perform led her to give her intended husband one month to consider whether he would accept a wife who would make all sacrifices to carry into effect her public duties.[34] It is easy to imagine that Archibald was surprised by Caroline's reaction to his proposal.

She was acting contrary to the advice of the time. Mrs Ellis, a popular writer of the period, wrote that the ideal for a wife was 'softness and weakness, delicacy and modesty, a small waist and curving shoulders, an endearing ignorance of everything that went on beyond household and social life'.[35] Caroline seems to have ignored Ellis's dictate to 'deny her feelings, and conceal her talents'.

That Archibald was ten years older than Caroline was not unusual.[36] There are many nineteenth-century novels that relate similar age gaps, which suggests the novelists were reflecting real life. Emilia Dilke wrote a number of stories of young women who marry professors.[37] Charlotte Brontë wrote in the same vein, particularly in *The Professor*, but also in *Villette* and *Shirley*. In *Middlemarch* George Eliot marries the young Dorothea Brooke to the older Mr Casaubon, in the hope that a 'fuller life would open up before her' and that she would 'enter on a higher grade of initiation'. Dorothea would have 'room for the energies which stirred uneasily under the dimness and pressure of her own ignorance and the petty peremptoriness of the world's habits'.[38] What these novels have in common is the 'tutelary quality of such marriages' and the 'considerable age differences between the partners'.[39] Caroline may have chosen Archibald because she saw his army career as widening her own horizons, and his higher social standing as an opportunity to undertake a wider sphere of philanthropic works.

Archibald would no doubt have been aware that accepting 'a wife who would make all sacrifices to carry into effect her public duties' would make life difficult for himself. In the nineteenth century it was believed that a woman's place should be confined to the private sphere. Having a wife who entered the public sphere would have made their marriage most unconventional.

Archibald agreed to Caroline's request, however, and the wedding took place by special licence at the Church of the Holy Sepulchre, Northampton, on 27 December 1830. Caroline's sister Charlotte and Charlotte's stepdaughter Frances signed the marriage register.[40] The Reverend Spencer Gunning, by permission of the Reverend Benjamin Winthrop, officiated. Reverend Gunning's brother, John, served with the Madras Infantry.[41] As John was appointed cadet in 1818, the same year as Archibald, he would have known Archibald, and this is possibly the reason Reverend Gunning was asked to officiate instead of Reverend Winthrop, the then incumbent of the church. The East India Company army records indicate that Archibald and John did not serve in the same regiment, but they would have socialised at Fort St George. A friendship between the two men might explain Archibald's return to Northampton in 1828.

Although Archibald was a Roman Catholic it was a legal requirement that the wedding take place in an Anglican church. The Catholic clergy were not legally empowered to hold and register wedding services.

It is believed that Caroline converted to Catholicism at this time. Her conversion to her husband's faith should not be viewed lightly. In view of the continued feeling against members of the Roman Catholic faith, it was a significant decision.

The fear, hostility and intensity of ill-will toward the Roman Catholic Church and its adherents dated back to Tudor times and the beginning of the Church of England. The minority who remained faithful to the Church of Rome often found themselves looked upon with suspicion and were denied many civil rights. The Catholic Relief Act of 1778 began the struggle for complete Catholic emancipation. The Act abolished the reward of £100 to informers against priests and schoolmasters and abolished the punishment of perpetual imprisonment. The 1581 Act against saying or hearing Mass still remained in force. The Relief Act permitted Catholics to hold property and to acquire it by purchase or inheritance, and it abolished the right of the nearest Protestant heir to lay claim to the estates of his Catholic parents or relatives. Catholics were still exposed to severe penalties for some religious ceremonies and education was restricted. They were excluded from the House of Lords, from the House of Commons, from becoming servants of the crown, from the bar, from the exercise of the parliamentary franchise, and from commissions in the army and navy. The Act still contained clauses regarding enrolment of estate deeds, and Catholics had to pay a double land tax.[42] Additional relief was granted in a further act in 1791.

The Act of Union in 1800 abolished the Irish parliament and gave Ireland one hundred members of parliament and twenty-eight representative peers in the parliament of the United Kingdom of Great Britain and Ireland at Westminster. The Act added to rather than solved Anglo-Irish problems. The Irish resented the loss of their parliament and were grieved that the Act did not remove the political disadvantages of Catholic Irishmen. Daniel O'Connell established the Catholic Association in 1823. His main aims were repeal of the union and the restoration of the parliament in Dublin. It was the possibility of revolution in Ireland that led to the Catholic Emancipation Act in 1829, enabling Catholics to vote, hold public office, sit in parliament and plead at the bar. There had been petitions and agitations throughout the period, which fuelled anti-Catholic feeling, notably the Gordon Riots of 1780.[43] Lord George Gordon, head of the Protestant Association in 1780, petitioned parliament to retain anti-Catholic laws. The House of Commons refused to debate the issue, the consequence of which was widespread rioting directed at Catholic shops and the homes of wealthy Catholics. There was arson and theft and the Bank of England was attacked. The government took its time calling in the troops to restore order. Approximately 700 people were killed and many properties destroyed.[44] The Catholics may have obtained emancipation, but it was not so easy to eradicate the feelings and habits induced by centuries of persecution.[45]

William Cobbett, a journalist and radical campaigner, wrote at length and with feeling on the subject. In May 1811 he published an article called 'Dissenters, Methodists and Catholics'. He recalled that the Reformation '*originated* not in any dislike on the part of the people to the tenets or ceremonies of the Catholic Church, but in the laziness, the neglects, and, in some cases, oppressions of the Clergy, aided by a quarrel between the King and the Pope'. He was dismayed and indignant when he heard a 'Churchman or a Dissenter abuse … the Catholics'. He was equally indignant when he heard a Dissenter and Methodist complain about persecution but join together to abuse Catholics and 'shut the Catholic out from political liberty on account of his religious tenets'. Cobbett felt it 'stupid as well as very insolent to talk in this way of the Catholics; to represent them as doomed to perdition, who compose five-sixths of the population of Europe'.[46]

One of the few working men's autobiographies, *The Autobiography of a Beggar Boy* by James Dawson Burn, first published in 1855, shows quite clearly how the detail above would have affected a Catholic in reality. He recalls the attitude toward members of the Roman Catholic faith during the early part of the nineteenth century. He writes of his stepfather's faith and gives a very descriptive view of the intolerance that members of the Catholic Church had to contend with. He wrote:

> It will be remembered that people professing Catholicism in those days were marked with the hateful *brand* of the national stigma. They were therefore continually labouring under a painful sense of their unmerited wrongs. The members of the Church of Rome, though British subjects, and contributing to the national wealth, and submitting to all the conditions of society, were debarred nearly all the rights and privileges of common citizens. They were not only continually subject to the gross and brutal attacks of the ignorant, but their wrongs were frequently used as stepping-stones to state preferment by the rich and powerful. It was thus that the deadly embers of religious animosity were kept alive, and one class of society was continually made the foot-ball of the other. I have no doubt but my step-father's mind must have been soured by the overbearing conduct of his comrades while in the army, who took occasion to prove their sense of religion by a system of heartless persecution, which was at that time sure to find favour with their superiors.[47]

That Burn's step-father faced religious persecution in the army, presumably the British army, raises the question as to whether Archibald suffered the same fate in the East India Company army, and whether Caroline, as the captain's wife, experienced the same difficulties.

Burn later writes of the passing of the Emancipation Act. He saw the year 1829 'as one of the most eventful in the history of the first half of the nineteenth century'. He emphasised that for:

> a great portion of this year, the whole country was in an alarming state of excitement. The labours of the Catholic Association were about producing their desired effect. The Duke of Wellington and Sir Robert Peel had opposed the Catholic claims with all the moral force they could bring to bear upon the question; but at length, seeing those claims could be no longer resisted with safety to the state, they made a virtue of necessity, and carried the measure, in the face of taunts and vollies of abuse from their former colleagues. During six months, the Anti-Catholic spirit was in a continual state of effervescence; and petitions and counter-petitions were poured into the Houses of Parliament in wagon-loads. All the trickery of low cunning, and the malignancy of sectarian zeal, with no small portion of honest hatred, were brought to bear against the passing of this measure.[48]

Negative sentiments against Catholics continued well into the nineteenth century. In 1850 the Pope, for administrative purposes, decided to re-establish one metropolitan see and twelve suffragan bishoprics, amongst them Northampton.[49] Incensed, the Bishop of Durham wrote publicly to the Prime Minister, Lord John Russell, complaining of the 'insolent and insidious' nature of the 'Papal Aggression' implied by the creation of the Catholic hierarchy. The Prime Minister replied in *The Times* on 7 November 1850, agreeing with the Bishop in considering 'the late aggression of the Pope upon our Protestantism [as] insolent and insidious'.[50]

New converts to Rome were popularly called perverts rather than converts. Gladstone saw his sister Helen's conversion to Rome as 'the record of our shame' and urged his father to expel her from the family home. Three of the four sons of William Wilberforce converted to Rome, and the remaining son, the Anglican Samuel Wilberforce, Bishop of Oxford, 'heartily wished his brother Henry would settle abroad'. Samuel stated that 'having him here after this dreadful fall seems to me beyond measure miserable; and his broken vows and violated faith weigh heavily on my soul. May God forgive him.'[51]

Caroline's own family seems not to have reacted quite as strongly. The will of Caroline's sister Harriet indicates not only that the families were in contact with one another, but that Harriet, who was involved with the Wesleyan Chapel, had no qualms in making a financial bequest from the sale of three properties in Great Russell Street, Northampton, to her Catholic nephew, Henry Chisholm, and her niece Charlotte, the wife of Reverend John Broad, who spent seven years as curate at All Saints, Northampton.[52] The will demonstrates the Jones family's broad-mindedness as opposed to Victorian bigotry, suggesting Caroline and her siblings were brought up within an enlightened atmosphere.

The *Northampton Mercury* of Saturday, 5 April 1828 carried an advertisement that amply demonstrates the anti-Catholic feelings within the town. It was placed by the Archdeacon of Northampton and informed the clergy of the diocese of Peterborough that petitions to both Houses of Parliament against further concessions to the Roman Catholics were available for signature at nine homes within Northamptonshire, as well as at the registrar's offices in Northampton and Peterborough. The Northampton Religious and Useful Knowledge Society was founded in 1839 specifically to combat popery and infidelity by challenging the local Mechanics Institution. In the early 1850s the local Conservative leader, John Palmer Kilpin, circulated a rumour about a poor servant girl whose conversion to Roman Catholicism had allegedly driven her mad.[53] Interestingly, when the *Northampton Mercury* reported a meeting that Caroline held in Northampton in 1853 they noted that Mrs Chisholm was expected to revisit the town and she had been requested to give some information to the Religious and Useful Knowledge Society.[54]

Northampton celebrated Guy Fawkes Night in 1850 to a far greater extent than it had done so in the past. The *Northampton Herald* reported 'the feeling of Northampton against Popery, and the chance of a return to the darkness of past ages, may be judged of by the displays on Tuesday, the hopes of the "Holy Father" cannot be of a very sanguine kind'.[55] Guy Fawkes Day was once the most important holiday in England and thus the most common expression of anti-Catholicism. That the people of Northampton chose to celebrate the occasion with fires in the streets (in the grounds of the churches, as previously) indicates a rise in anti-Catholic feelings.[56]

Caroline's decision to convert to her husband's faith seems to indicate a love for her husband and a courageous spirit. Throughout her working life her adopted faith would cause her considerable difficulty.

Following their marriage the couple spent some time in Brighton, but by 1831 they were back in Northampton living in Leicester Terrace. As with other members of the Jones family they resided within easy walking distance of each other. As Caroline was expecting the birth of their first child at the beginning of October, being near to her mother would have been a great comfort. Archibald extended his furlough on 23 February 1831 and again on 8 June for further periods of six months, and was with his wife for the birth of their first child.

In the last weeks of Caroline's confinement, the *Northampton Mercury* of 23 September 1831 carried reports of the petitions and counter-petitions regarding the Second Reform Bill passing to the House of Lords. The bill was introduced in February 1830 to abolish all rotten boroughs with their transfer to the counties and large towns. It was also proposed that the maximum parliamentary life should be five years, MPs should be paid with a household franchise in the boroughs, and that the county franchise should be extended to include copyholders, who held land by custom without formally owning it.[57] There were many working men who believed it to be unjust that they should not have a vote, and they sought representation so that they could draw attention to their economic grievances.[58] The bill was rejected in the early hours of 8 October 1831 by a majority of forty-one.

Riots broke out in Derby and Nottingham and continued for the rest of the month. There were also riots in other large towns, particularly Bristol, and in the smaller, west of England woollen towns, such as Blandford and Tiverton.[59] Caroline's daughter, also named Caroline, was born in the first week, but died at three weeks and was buried on 26 October at St Sepulchre's Church. Caroline and Archibald were aware of the disturbances. In 1842, in the first year's *Report of the Sydney Immigrants' Home*, she referred to the breaking of the windows at the Mansion House in Bristol as a 'Bristol tune'.[60]

Caroline was still in England when King William IV gave his royal assent to the first Reform Act on 7 June 1832. Archibald had been back in India for nearly six months. The passing of the Act was a backward move for Northampton voters. Between 1768 and 1796 all male householders not in receipt of poor relief were entitled to vote, a wide franchise that the town retained until 1832. The Act imposed a uniform franchise on borough electorates and householders were rated at £10 or over. This reduced the number of persons in Northampton who were entitled to vote. Nearly 2,500 votes were polled at the election of 1831, but in 1852 there were only 1,815 names on the electoral roll, though the town had almost doubled in size during the intervening period.[61] The passing of the Act was a step forward for Scotland—it meant that there was a real prospect of elections in Scotland, though only one male in eight had the vote. Only five per cent of Irishmen were entitled to vote following the passing of the Act. Prime Minister Earl Grey, who was against annual parliaments, universal suffrage and the ballot, was convinced that moderate reform was the only secure route to political stability and a way of averting revolution in England.[62]

Caroline grew up during this period of transition and witnessed the development of steam engines and the construction of the railway system that transformed the countryside and altered the social and economic life of the British people. For many of the people, however, industrialisation did not bring with it a better lifestyle. It was in 1843 that Thomas Hood wrote the heart-rending poem 'The Song of the Shirt', attacking the use of sweated labour. This so affected Samuel Sidney Herbert that he was moved to inaugurate an emigration scheme to send young needlewomen to Australia. It was in 1847 that Caroline wrote of 'unparalleled misery and distress—at a time when England groans with the burden of her redundant population'.[63] She was well aware of the poverty that Henry Mayhew wrote about in *London Labour and the London Poor*. She could see for herself the duality of the destruction and reconstruction created by living in an age when change was revolutionary.

Archibald Chisholm as a young man. By kind permission of Don Chisholm

INDIA 1832–1838

Now married, the couple decided that Archibald should continue his service with the East India Company army. He had already extended his two-year furlough by just over a year, but in June 1831, when Caroline was three or four months' pregnant, he applied for a further six-month extension to his leave.

The idea of travelling to India with a three-month-old baby would not have been thought sensible, and obtaining a double berth for the journey to India together would have proved difficult and expensive. Sadly, the baby died. After only one year of married life the idea of separation must have dismayed the couple.

Archibald sailed on the *Elphinstone* from Gravesend on 6 January 1832. The ship, a sloop with eighteen guns, was captained by Mr J Short and arrived in Madras on 14 May 1832.[1] Places were limited and often allocated by a lottery system. At that time the fare would have been £100 or more. For that price the passenger would have a small cubicle or cabin that would have to be furnished, including bedding and linen. It would have been hazardous to walk the decks, which would have been strewn with pig-pens, chicken, geese and duck coops, and cow and sheep stalls.[2]

Travellers could use the alternative overland route, but it is debatable which would have been the more hazardous. The overland route may have been slightly shorter in duration, but far more exhausting.

Back in India, Archibald was given the commission of captain on 8 April 1833. That Archibald was able to speak 'Hindoostandee' would have helped his promotional prospects.[3] A captain's pay was £120 per annum, paid per month of thirty days, with £36 gratuity and £75 tent allowance. Archibald also received an allowance of £50 for horse rent if in receipt of half batta[4] and if he was not provided with quarters. Half batta was £90, giving a total of £371 per annum. When in the field the pay was £120 with £36 gratuity, £75 tent allowance, but no horse allowance, but £189 full batta, giving a total of £420 per annum.[5]

Before she left for India Caroline must have revisited the Brighton area, for among her miscellaneous papers at the State Library of New South Wales is a copy of a phrenological examination by Mr James De Ville of Brighton, dated 30 January 1833.[6] Possibly Archibald and Caroline had friends or family in Brighton, hence their visit there after their marriage in December 1830.

Phrenology was popular in the first half of the nineteenth century. We would think of phrenology today as 'bump reading'—reading the contours of the skull to obtain insight into a person's character. De Ville lived, worked and lectured in London, but undertook lectures at several public institutions outside the city. Caroline's phrenological report would appear, remarkably, to be fairly accurate. De Ville notes that Caroline's 'memory is rather extraordinary', she has a 'high sense of Religion' and 'theology must have undergone a good deal of consideration'. Caroline had 'a severe struggle with herself and inward feelings' and was 'kind and benevolent as far as her means go: love of children strongly developed'. As we will see later, she did indeed struggle with 'inward feelings' and had a strongly developed love of children. The Chisholms were in financial difficulties for most of their lives together, and De Ville's belief that Caroline was 'kind and benevolent as far as her means go' was quite accurate. He also wrote, 'give her the subject, and she will make you a speech on it, or write sheets full'. In later life Caroline wrote numerous letters to the press and many pamphlets. De Ville believed that Caroline had 'a gigantic organisation, more powerful than that of the Marquis Mascati', which also seems accurate. Caroline's organisational ability can be seen from her work for the Family Colonisation Loan Society.

Caroline sailed on the *Elphinstone* on 30 March 1833 and arrived in Madras on 4 August 1833. There were eight passengers.[7] A father writing to his daughters in 1820 before they left England for India gave strict guidelines for their safety, conduct and protection. He saw their life on board ship as fraught with difficulties, 'more especially of consequence when it is considered that you will meet persons whose character, morals and behaviour you are unacquainted with'.[8] He was also concerned that the girls should be properly dressed at all times; for decorum's sake, on no account were they to hang washing out to dry outside the cabin.[9] And even when they reached Madras, a welcome sight after three or four months on the high seas, they faced the dangers of getting ashore. Cumming, who arrived at the end of May 1837, wrote, 'We are now snugly anchored off Madras roads though there is a fearful surf on the beach', which prevented his landing for three days. 'Indeed on Sunday two gentlemen lost their lives and one lady was much injured.'[10]

It is not clear from Archibald's service record whether he was at Madras to greet his wife. If he had not been given leave, Caroline would have had to travel to Vellore alone, some thirty-five miles west of Madras, where Archibald was serving with the regiment.

The transition from a young woman in Northampton to the wife of an army captain in India would not have been easy for Caroline. She would have had to re-adjust to married life again after over eighteen months' separation and acclimatise herself to the weather and social niceties of living within the British community in India. Harriet Tytler, who was in India for thirty years from 1828, believed that it was the heat, added to the lack of any great necessity for action, that was the downfall of so many English ladies in India.[11] The normal routine for a memsahib was to rise between four and five to attend to household matters, followed perhaps by a short ride around the station before breakfast at eight. (It must have been at this time that Caroline learnt to ride. Such an accomplishment was to be of great benefit to her in her work in Australia.) There would be visits by ladies of the same social standing during the late morning and early afternoon; lunch would follow, and then a sleep through the heat in the whitewashed room of a screen-darkened bungalow. There would be an early evening drive and more socialising before returning home for dinner and an early night, if there were no plans to dine out. Children would have ayahs to care for them, and there would have been servants to run the household. Caroline was not used to dealing with servants, and it would not have been easy for her to fit into the 'glitter and enchantment of military life'.[12] As the wife of a company captain she would have been expected to follow a strict code of conduct—the wives of other ranks were referred to as 'women' and only mixed with very occasionally.

Caroline and Archibald's first son, Archibald, was born in Madras on 4 May 1836. The baby was less than two months old when the family set off at the end of June 1836 to the military station at Secunderabad, 394 miles to the north of Madras, just north-west of Hyderabad. Caroline may have opted out of travelling on horseback and lain in a palanquin with baby Archibald.[13]

Their second son, William, named after his maternal grandfather, was born at Bowenpilly on 6 September 1837. Bowenpilly was within the Secunderabad province, but not one of the outposts of the company. Possibly the baby had arrived early while she was returning to Madras, or the Chisholms had accommodation at Bowenpilly.[14]

It is difficult to imagine that Caroline established the Female School of Industry for the Daughters of European Soldiers in Madras whilst accompanying Archibald around India and giving birth to two sons. It is likely that she began organising the school a few years after her arrival in India, once she had made contacts and become acquainted with colonial life.

Caroline had observed children running wild within the barracks, and seen the lack of provision for the European soldiers' wives and children. The boys would be drafted into the army with their fathers but girls were left to their own devices. Mackenzie wrote of the 'familiarity with licentious and profane expressions, and indecorous conduct [that] must obliterate all delicacy of mind and action' in the female youth.[15] Caroline saw this and set about organising a girls' school.

The records of the Beckett and Sergeant Charity School in Northampton show a marked similarity to the school organised by Caroline in Madras. The school taught not only the three Rs, but also the domestic accomplishments of cookery, needlework, knitting and laundry skills. Religious instruction and moral conduct were also of particular importance. There is no record of Caroline being a pupil or teacher at the school in Northampton, but she may have been aware of its methods, and of the Schools of Industry in England which 'catered for girls of lower socio-economic background ... where girls ... spent most of their time learning domestic skills in preparation for service and marriage and motherhood'.[16]

To organise and run such a school Caroline needed financial support. She was able to raise 2,000 rupees quickly, and the Governor of Madras, Lieutenant General Sir Frederick Adams, gave £20.[17] The school was allocated a room within Fort St George, but then moved to Black Town to escape the barracks' influence. Mackenzie suggests that the move isolated the Chisholms as Black Town was considered unhealthy and unfashionable by the officers and their wives.[18]

The girls learnt their lessons through practical achievements. They were encouraged to be industrious, to take pride in themselves and to consider how proud their parents would be of them. They kept strict records of expenditure, cared for their sick friends and had to account for any wastage. The water used to boil barley, for instance, was not thrown away but put to good use.[19] Wastage was seen as particularly sinful in Victorian times. The rules of the school show Caroline's practical nature and her understanding of the difficulties of parents who were not so well off.

While religious instruction was important, no one religion was favoured, foreshadowing Caroline's determination 'to serve all creeds' at her Immigrants' Home in Australia. The girls could acquire tickets for good behaviour and the child who had obtained the most was awarded a prize. The hard-won tickets could easily be lost. Telling an untruth led to the forfeiture of five tickets and isolation from the other children. A child caught stealing, however trifling the offence, would also have five tickets deducted and be separated from her classmates. For a second offence, the child would be made to wear a black bracelet, making her offence highly visible. All bad behaviour was entered in a black book which was shown to visitors and parents; it was emphasised to the child the distress that such an entry would cause. The rod was to be used only as a last resort.

The school was a success, so much so that young mothers begged to join the classes. Young non-commissioned officers sought wives and servants from the young girls who had completed their education at the school. Caroline continued to oversee the school while looking after her own two sons and travelling with Archibald. She wrote an 'Address to be read by the Mistress' and an 'Address to the Matron and the Mistress', to be read in her absence, as detailed by Mackenzie in *Memoirs*.

In the address to be read by the mistress, Caroline hoped that 'My dear little Girls' would 'look upon the Bracelets with a determination never to wear them', and assured the students that it was 'much easier to be good than to be bad, and you must be one or the other'. She told the girls that if they lied they would soon 'learn to steal, for one generally follows the other; and if you steal sugar and little things, I fear you will in time steal broaches, and I dread to think what your end may be'. The girls were told not to forget the kindness of their parents in placing them in a situation where they were not surrounded by vice and wickedness, and were charged to show their gratitude by their good conduct, and learn to be useful, so they might be 'hereafter' of 'real use' to their parents.

The lack of diaries and letters written by Caroline at this time makes it difficult to ascertain exactly where she obtained the idea, motivation and strength for setting up the school. It is possible that she helped run a school in Northampton, but this is speculation; there is no documentation to support the suggestion.

The *Madras Almanac and Compendium of Intelligence for 1842* shows that a Ladies Institution for the Education of the Daughters of Europeans and their Descendants in the Presidency of Madras was still in operation at this time. A ladies' committee ran the school and it was reported that 'the School in connection with this Institution has been removed to the large and commodious house formerly occupied by the late Dr Bannister, at Vepery'. A day school had also been opened in Popham's Broadway, Black Town, and placed under the care of a Miss Austen. Mackenzie's biographies suggest that the Female School of Industry in Madras, at the time of his writing around 1852, had become an 'extensive orphanage'. An article written in *The Tablet* on 19 June 1909 indicates that the school was still in existence at that date. There is no indication that Caroline was in communication with the school after she left India.

Archibald returned to the Presidency of Madras on 15 January 1838, where he applied in writing, enclosing his medical certificate, for permission to proceed to New South Wales and Van Diemen's Land on 9 February 1838. The records do not give the reason for Archibald's medical certification, but the surgeons John Wylie and R. Cole note that Captain Chisholm was 'in a bad state of health' and they thought it 'necessary that he should be permitted to proceed to New South Wales for the recovery of his health, with leave of absence for two years'. Archibald had served a total of seventeen years in India and, as was a common occurrence, his health had suffered. Leave was duly recommended by the Commander in Chief and signed by B. R. Hitchins, Adjutant General of the Army, and the order given on 12 February 1838.[20]

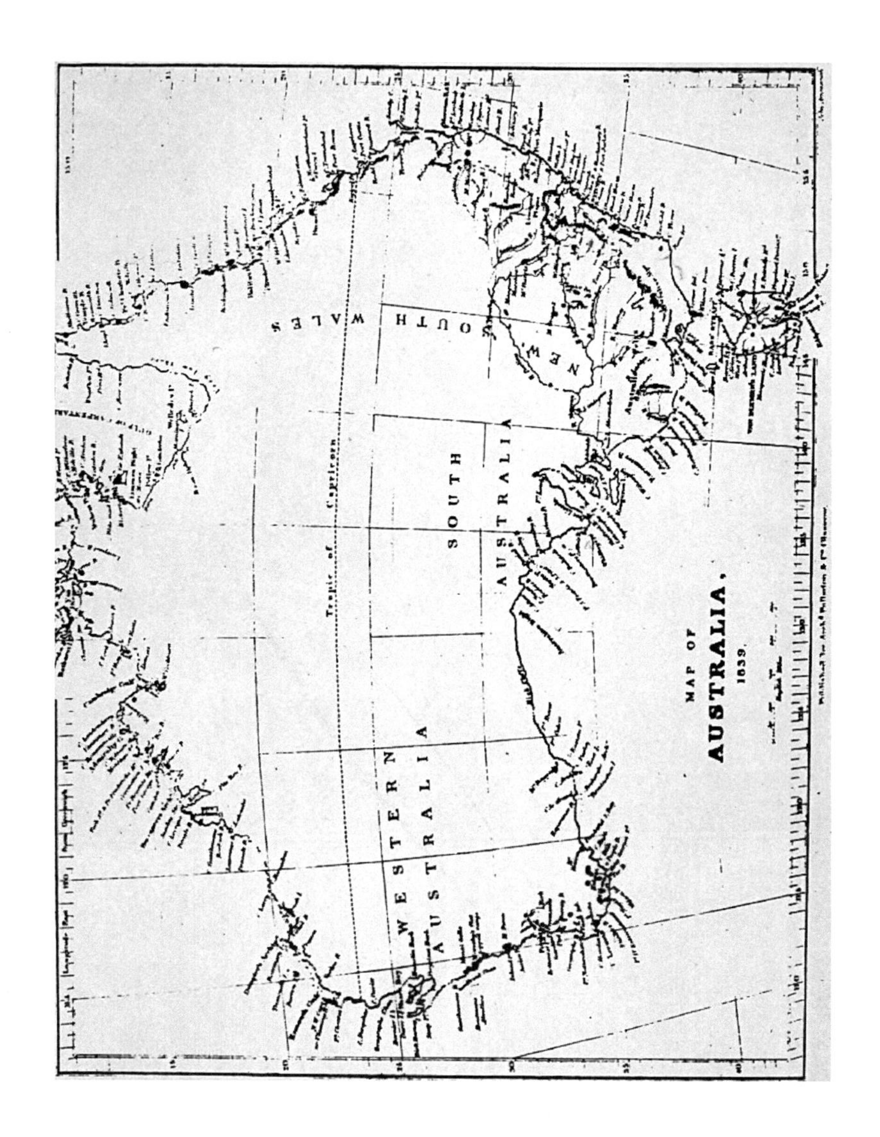

Map of Australia, 1839

AUSTRALIA AND EMIGRATION 1838–1846

During her time in India Caroline had come to terms with the oppressive heat, the strict social hierarchy within the Company army's establishment at Madras and the imperial attitudes towards Indians. Like their Queen, Victorians viewed the Empire as a possession, if a worrisome one.

Expressions of concern over imperial behaviour were not, however, uncommon. On his tour of India in 1875, the Prince of Wales wrote home to his mother expressing his conviction that Indians of all classes would 'be more attached to us if treated with kindness and with firmness ... but not with brutality or contempt'.[1]

Upon their arrival in Australia, the differences between their new home and India would have been apparent to Caroline and Archibald. Britain's approach to the two colonies differed—emigration being at the root of that difference. In India the native population was to be ruled, but in Australia there was a sense that the Aborigines were different and should not be too much interfered with.[2] British settlement of Australia began in the late eighteenth century as a penal colony, a replacement for the now-lost penal establishments in America.[3] At the time of the Chisholms' arrival, the New South Wales colony was accepting free settlers and Australia was beginning to be seen as a place where, given the right balance between land, labour and capital, the white working-class emigrant would prosper, enabling the production of raw materials for British manufacture. Those same prosperous workers would, in turn, provide an enthusiastic market for British goods, and British wealth would circulate throughout the Empire.[4]

Towards the end of the eighteenth century the increasing population in Britain led Thomas Malthus, a clergyman and mathematician, to ponder the problem of the dramatic rise in population without the equivalent rise in food production. His solution was to discourage relationships that would produce children and to encourage emigration. He realised that the poor could not emigrate without financial assistance. Parliament was not enthusiastic, however, with the proposal put forward early in the nineteenth century to fund emigration from the poor rate. Likewise there was little enthusiasm for the proposal to seek contributions from landlords in Scotland and Ireland. It was suggested that the emigrant be given free land, but after four years' settlement they would be required to repay the loan. Malthus stated that nobody should be compelled to go overseas, but that if they did refuse to go they should be denied poor relief.

In 1828 Wilmot Horton introduced a bill in Parliament that would allow parishes to mortgage their poor rates to provide for their able-bodied paupers to emigrate to the British colonies. Horton's bill suggested that the paupers should be supplied with goods to enable them to settle and to make something of their lives, rather than be a burden. The bill was defeated, and again in 1830. However, Horton was involved with experimental emigration to Canada to assist unemployed Irish labourers. The scheme was successful, but not repeated because of the excessive costs involved.[5] In 1832 the government made it clear that they did not intend to give monetary assistance to those who wished to emigrate but five years later such assistance was available.

There are similarities between the emigration schemes suggested by Horton and Edward Gibbon Wakefield. They both foresaw that the poor could be turned into a labour force, although they differed in their views as to how that end might be reached. The fear that the 'propertyless masses' might revolt drew support for Wakefield's systematic colonisation as a means of 'diffusing discontent while creating new fields of opportunity for paupers abroad'.[6] Wakefield was an unusual, poorly educated character. While he was in prison (for abducting an under-aged heiress with the intention of marrying her) he read everything he could with regard to colonisation. His predicament did not stop him from publishing his views on emigration in a paper called *A Letter from Sydney*, which was published in 1829. He used the pen name of Roger Gouger, pretending he was a struggling emigrant in New South Wales. Four years later, under his own name, he published *The Art of Colonisation.*

Wakefield's systematic colonisation was founded on the premise that emigration should work on the principle of supply and demand, and that land should not be given free of charge. Land should be sold at a fixed price per acre. This would, he felt, improve the character of those going to the colonies. It would encourage those who were prepared to work to establish themselves, and discourage the impoverished, the idle and the infirm. In a *Letter from Sydney*, he noted the lack of paid labourers available to develop the rich resources of the colony. Land had been too easy to obtain, and those who had risked the long journey to an unknown land did not want to work for anybody other than themselves. Wakefield believed his system of emigration would redress the balance. Caroline's strong dislike for the

Wakefield system of colonisation may well have stemmed from her time spent in Adelaide during her voyage to Australia on the *Emerald Isle*. She would have been able to observe at first-hand some of the problems of the Wakefield system, the confusion and speculation over the price of land, and the high price of labour, in the newly founded colony of South Australia.

Studies show that 'although poor, sometimes from the very margins of the economy, government emigrants bound for Australia were, typically, literate, enterprising, self-selecting individuals who sought opportunities to exchange lives of under-employment at home in an unstable socio-economic environment, for the chance of full employment in the colonies where their labour was in demand'.[7] It was not just the conditions at home that made people feel that they had no alternative but to emigrate, or, later, the allure of the goldfields and the belief that life could be better overseas. The decision to go was as much about friends and relatives asking, begging or paying emigrants to join them in their new homeland. Emigration 'tended to run in families'.[8]

Between 1809 and 1820 Governor Macquarie further developed the physical structure of Sydney and helped change the martial settlement to a civic community, but quarrels between him and his officials resulted in his recall by home government. Although there had been a depression in Sydney from 1822 to 1825, the town continued to prosper. The Bank of New South Wales was established, and a new legal system with trial by jury had been put in place. There were also improvements to the water supply, and improvements made in the educational system. A Legislative Council was set up and the agitation for responsible government began. Sydney also boasted a number of newspapers with freedom of the press.

Samuel Sidney, writing of Sydney before the great crash of 1843, found Australia the most hospitable country in the world. He went on to say 'the streets of Sydney were particularly brilliant' with 'landaus, gigs, all kinds of quiet carriages, and ladies and gentlemen on horseback'. He noted 'among the goverment clerks and the sons of wealthy emancipists that there were great numbers of both sexes who delighted to adorn themselves after the exact pattern of the book of fashions',[9] though a banker giving Sidney advice suggested that the 'topping citizens of Sydney very much resemble the same gentlemen in Manchester; they are so busy making money, that unless you have a large letter of credit they have no time to be hospitable to you, in fact, they can't afford it'.

Caroline and Archibald and their two small sons embarked on the 551-ton *Emerald Isle* from Madras on 23 March 1838. They travelled with three native servants, who returned to India after the completion of the journey.[10] The ship was grossly overloaded, and it had to put in for repairs at Mauritius for a month. It was further delayed for a month at Adelaide, and three weeks at Hobart Town, before sailing on to Sydney. The journey took seven months and it would have given Caroline an insight into the needs of emigrants on board ship that she would use later when making plans for the Family Colonisation Loan Society ships sailing for Australia.

New South Wales had enjoyed several years of real prosperity, but when Caroline and Archibald arrived Sydney was facing a financial crisis.[11] Prosperity had been based on the anticipation of extraordinary returns from the investment of funds borrowed mainly from English capitalists at an exorbitant rate of interest and spent on ruinous speculations in land and stock. There had been extraordinary inflation followed by a 'deep and general depression', and then a 'state of collapse'. The 'whole framework of society' had been affected by the horrendous downward turn in the economy.[12] The Bank of Australia failed and it was estimated that there were nearly 'sixteen hundred and forty bankruptcies both in town and country'.[13] As a consequence, there was a glut of sheep, which sold for as little as sixpence a head, and land sales ceased. The labour market was overstocked and made worse by the influx of penniless immigrants, who were being brought out to Australia under the bounty system. This system of immigration had been conceived during the period of prosperity, but was being operated in the climate of depression.[14] Colonial government did little to help the immigrants, except to erect an Immigration Barracks in Phillip Street.

After their arrival in Sydney in October 1838, Archibald and Caroline and their two sons settled in a cottage in Windsor on the Hawkesbury River, some thirty miles inland to the north-west of Sydney, a 'wearisome drive of five or six hours'.[15] As a Scot, Archibald was 'acutely aware of the value of education' and regarded a school as an essential element in a community. It was an idea Archibald would have 'carried with him wherever he went',[16] and may well account for the choice of Windsor as a home.

The town had a good few houses, a court house, a benevolent asylum and a branch of the Commercial Bank. There was also a police magistrate and a solicitor. A small settlement of Aborigines lived just outside the town. There was a Roman Catholic school in George Street, conducted by James and Esther Cassidy from 1835 to 1844 with 104 scholars on the roll in 1838.[17] In 1837 there was only one religious building in the town, that of the Church of England, compared to about forty public houses, 'quite out of proportion to the extent and requirements of the place', including one called Help me through the World.[18] The Roman Catholics met in a room or shed in Macquarie Street belonging to a Mrs Christopher Davis. The resident priest was the Reverend Father Brady.[19] The Catholics eventually acquired their own church, opened by Archbishop Polding on 21 October 1840 with the assistance of Reverend W. Ullathorne.

It was during expeditions from Windsor to Sydney that Caroline and Archibald first became aware of the unacceptable conditions that faced newly arrived immigrants. Many immigrants, like Henry Parkes and his family, arrived with little or no money and without the prospect of employment. Parkes and his wife, Clarinda, and their newborn baby, were bounty immigrants who arrived on the *Strathfieldsaye* in 1839, ten months after the Chisholms. Parkes 'sold some of their little stock to help support the family' and at 'length being completely starved out' he engaged as a 'common labourer about thirty-six miles up the country ... at £25 per annum with a ration and a half of food'. Parkes was very disappointed with Australia. In a letter home, written in May 1840, he said he found it difficult to write of the wickedness he found in his new homeland. For the first four months he and his family lived in a very poorly appointed hut. He did not even have the opportunity to provide home grown vegetables for the family, for 'the slave-masters of NSW require their servants to work for them from sunrise till sunset, and will not allow them to have gardens, lest they should steal a half-hour's time to work in them'. Not surprisingly, he finishes his letter home by saying that 'not one of his companions that travelled out with him on the *Strathfieldsaye* but most heartily wished to be back home'.[20]

It is doubtful that the poor who had travelled on the *Strathfieldsaye* really would have wished to go home to live under the English Poor Law.

The fundamental principles of the new Poor Law of 1834 were the refusal of poor relief to the able-bodied, and for the relief to be at a rate below that of the poorest independent worker. For the weak and helpless, all relief would be channelled into a workhouse. This was an endeavour to stop fraud and to encourage a return to normal work at the first opportunity.[21] There was considerable resentment of the English Poor Law in Australia. The Australians did not 'want a Poor Law Tax or their poor to be treated like outcasts in State Institutions'.[22] Attempts were made to create a relief system more congenial to the Australian mentality.

Around 1832, large numbers of emigrants in similar situations to Henry Parkes and his family began to arrive in the colony under the system of assisted immigration. They often sought help from the Asylum in cases of sickness, homelessness or other, mostly temporary, needs. To help immigrants arriving in the colony a Roman Catholic Relief Society—the Strangers' Friend Society—was formed in 1835 along similar lines to the outdoor relief branch of the Benevolent Society. The first single females sent to Australia arrived in 1832 and were welcomed and cared for by a Ladies' Committee. By 1838 the sheer number of single females arriving in Sydney, destitute and alone and unable to find work, was considerable. The Ladies' Committee found it impossible to care for such large numbers of women. In July 1839 the Sydney Association for the Temporary Relief of the Poor was founded. It raised subscriptions to buy meat, oatmeal, sugar, rice, sago and other foodstuff, and fuel. It then sold the items at reduced prices to the poor.[23]

In 1826 Mrs Darling, the Governor's wife, founded a Female School of Industry to train girls to do the work of servants. The school was organised and maintained by private subscription. The school initially opened with twenty pupils; numbers were often under thirty and rarely exceeded forty. The school remained open until 1926.[24] Mrs Darling was also involved in attempts to establish a Ladies' Committee for the Female Factory at Parramatta. The factory was a prison, with nearly one thousand convicts in 1839, as well as a workhouse, a house of correction and a hospital. It had a bad reputation. The ladies of Sydney and Parramatta found the charitable work unpalatable and the Committee only operated for a short period of time.[25]

This was the state of immigration in Sydney when Caroline and Archibald arrived. On one occasion they came across some 'Highland emigrants, who only spoke Gaelic, had large families, and found difficulty in obtaining employment. A little money lent them by Captain Chisholm to purchase tools, and a little useful advice, set them up as wood-cutters, and they prospered'.[26] But Caroline was particularly concerned with the plight of young girls who 'were ... sent ... without friends or advisers'. As Samuel Sidney suggested, it was the 'unprotected position of female and often friendless emigrants that awakened Caroline's warmest sympathies'.[27] She 'observed that many of them did not conduct themselves with propriety'.[28] Caroline was aware that the young girls were prey to the dubious attentions of men. She visited the immigrants' barracks in Sydney and was surprised to learn that there was a ladies' committee but that the ladies never visited the building. It was after this visit that Caroline devoted all her 'leisure time in endeavouring to serve these poor girls, and felt determined, with God's blessing, never to rest until *decent protection* was afforded them'. Caroline initially sheltered the young girls in her home—up to as many as nine at one time.[29]

For Caroline it was the plight of Flora, a beautiful Highland girl who had been seduced by a married gentleman and was contemplating suicide, that convinced Caroline that 'the evil which struck me so forcibly would soon be made apparent to the good people of Sydney' and spurred her on to 'serve these poor girls'. [30] Caroline particularly abhored and loathed the way single women were shipped out to Australia under the bounty system. In this she was not alone. In May 1851, Charles Dickens's *Household Words* carried a very strongly worded article on the 'Safety for Female Emigrants'.

Just a year after they had settled in Windsor, another son, Henry John, was born to Caroline and Archibald on 30 July 1839. He was baptised at St Mary's Church in Sydney on 7 August 1839. Later that year Archibald was recalled to active service and in January 1840 he sailed for India alone. They had concluded that it would be 'more prudent for the health of the family that Caroline remain for some time longer in the more favourable climate of Sydney'.[31]

Archibald arrived in India in March 1840[32] and only eight months later on 24 November requested that he should be 'disqualified for active duties of his profession ... at his own request, transferred to the Invalid Establishment'.[33] Archibald was posted to the 2nd Native Veteran Battalion and continued to serve in India until his retirement from the Service on 5 June 1845.[34]

Eneas Mackenzie believed that Archibald returned to India on his own for the health of the family and so that Caroline could stay and carry out philanthropic works. He stated in his inimitable style:

> ... the devoted and noble minded husband urged his beloved and courageous wife to carry out those views over which they had pondered for the reformation of evils detrimental to morality, the success of the

colony, the honour of their native country, and the mission of man on earth.[35]

Samuel Sidney, in a down-to-earth manner, related that it was Chisholm who first pointed out to his wife that the 'neglected state of the bounty emigrants … [were] fit objects for her charitable zeal and energy'.[36]

Against this background Caroline began what many have called her social work.[37] In January 1841 Caroline wrote to Lady Gipps to seek her help in founding the Sydney Immigrants' Home, and from that day onward she never ceased in her exertions.[38] She enquired 'if *any* ladies felt an interest in these young creatures [single female immigrants], or afforded them protection?' She was told 'there was a committee, but the ladies never visited the institute [immigration barracks] or interfered',[39] she contacted the 'ladies who formed the committee', seeking assistance, and was pleased that 'no one refused her'. Lady Gipps gave Caroline kind and generous support, and 'strewed a few flowers' in her path by helping her gain access to Governor George Gipps.

Organising, funding and arranging accommodation for these girls in Sydney was not an easy task for Caroline. The difficulties she faced and the deep humiliation she was made to feel on many occasions made Caroline 'suffer much', but as she wrote in *Female Immigration*:

On the Easter Sunday, I was enabled, at the altar of our Lord, to make an offering of my talents to the God who gave them. I promised to know *neither country or creed*, but to try and serve all *justly* and impartially. I asked only to be enabled to keep these poor girls from being tempted, by their need, to mortal sin; and resolved that, to accomplish this, I would in every

> way sacrifice my feelings—surrender all comfort—nor, in fact, consider my own wishes or feelings, but wholly devote myself to the work I had in hand. I felt my offering was accepted, and that God's blessing was on my work: but it was his will to permit many *serious difficulties* to be thrown in my way, and to conduct me through a rugged path of deep humiliation.[40]

Writing in 1967, T. R. Luscombe noted that the frequent repetition of this paragraph has robbed it of its true impact. But the quotation provides, as no other words can, the depth of religious feeling that inspired Caroline's selfless work.[41] Unfortunately, the difficulties thrown in her way arose because of her religion. There was 'a giving way—even some of my first promised supporters withdrew their pledges'. In *Female Immigration* she wrote:

> It is a remarkable fact, that, at the very time the Protestants were afraid of my 'Popish Plot', several of the leading Catholics had withdrawn their support; and I was daily and hourly requested to give up all thoughts of the 'Home'. A few dismal days passed; indeed, I had nothing to cheer me but an assurance of success, if there were no failing on my part: I could have done without help, but this continued opposition wearied me. Two gentlemen, one a clergyman, called on me; they urged me to give up.[42]

The Catholic clergy approved of the use of the barracks but were of the opinion that the clergymen and ministers of any denomination should not be expected to solicit subscriptions in their churches for the relief of emigrants, as had been proposed.[43] The clergy felt it was the duty of ship-owners and the government to support the emigrants until work was found. Caroline 'knew their [the clergy's] intentions were friendly towards' her, and she respected them, but she could not 'feel persuaded of their humanity or judgement'.[44]

Caroline would have found the continual opposition wearisome and been hurt by the wording of some of the letters she received. In *Female Immigration* she details her reaction to a letter from one of the clergy. It was 'of so painful a nature, that I am astonished how my mind held out: I felt a giving way of the body first; I found I should be driven from the field by those who ought to raise the standard and cry, "On, on!"'[45] Regrettably, she does not give any further information concerning this letter, but draws our attention to another letter, from Father Brennan, that was printed in *The Chronicle* on 16 September 1841, and was 'another blow … hurled against' her 'from the hand of a friend … a missile of great strength'.[46] She 'felt it keenly; no other person in the colony could have thrown more serious difficulties in my path: these things are *permitted* to try our faith and exercise our patience'. Father Brennan concluded his letter suggesting the:

> editors should unite to put the case to His Excellency and the Council, who he felt sure will not hesitate to relieve from want, and protect from vice, the poor but virtuous immigrant. It will be much better for you to do this than to waste your energies in endeavouring to promote a private scheme of benevolence, perfectly Utopian, and only excusable as the effect of an amiable delusion.[47]

One can understand why Caroline 'felt a dreariness of spirit creep over' her, to have her scheme referred to as an 'amiable delusion'. She thought it would be 'prudent to leave Sydney for a few days', but missed the steamer she was to catch. To Caroline, it seemed as if 'it was the will of God to prevent' her departure, as she subsequently came across 'the Highland beauty', Flora, who was contemplating suicide. She managed to talk Flora out of her plans and found her lodgings. Although Caroline was 'much tired and fatigued', her 'spirits returned: I felt God's blessing was on my work. From this time, I never thought of *human help;* I neglected no steps to conciliate; I increased my exertions; but from the hour I was on the beach with Flora, fear left me.'[48]

Even with the help of Lady Gipps, it still took Caroline some time to obtain help from the Governor, who believed she had 'over-rated the powers of her mind'. He eventually allowed her the use of the immigrants' barracks—'such a trifle ... so long withheld',[49] on the understanding that the Colonial Government would not be put to any expense. The home was to be run entirely on public subscription.

Not only was Caroline's determination and perseverance tested in her battle to acquire the barracks for the single women, her first night there also challenged her resolve. She wrote:

> On closing the door I reflected on what I had been compelled to endure for fourteen feet square: my first feelings were those of indignation that such a trifle should have been so long withheld; but better feelings followed: I determined on trusting to Providence to increase its size, and prove my usefulness ... I soon observed, to do any good, I must sleep on the premises; and, as soon as he [Mr Merewether, the Immigration Agent] was aware of my determination, he gave me the best room then vacant—I cannot say vacant, for it was used as a store-room: this was cleared for my

> accommodation; and having been busy all day, I retired wearied to rest. But I was put to the proof at starting: scarce was the light out, when I fancied a few dogs must be in the room, and, in some terror, I got a light; what I experienced on seeing rats in all directions I cannot explain. My first act was to throw on my cloak, and get at the door with the intent to leave the building: I knew if I did this my desertion would cause much amusement and ruin my plan: I therefore lighted a second candle, and seating myself on the bed, kept there until three rats, descending from the roof, alighted on my shoulders. I knew that I was getting into a fever, in fact, that I should be very ill before morning; but to be out-generalled by rats was too much. I got up with some resolution; I had two loaves and some butter (for my office, bed-room, and pantry, were one;) I cut it into slices, placed the whole in the middle of the room, put a dish of water convenient, and with a light by my side, I kept my seat on the bed … watching the rats until four in the morning: I at one time counted thirteen, and never less than seven did I observe at the dish during the night. The following night I gave them a similar treat with the addition of arsenic; and thus passed my four first nights at the Home.[59]

Sir George begrudgingly allowed Caroline the privileges of free postage, but even then he questioned the validity of the recipients. He felt she should just have been addressing the mail to the magistrates and police of the different districts, but she also wrote to the people she considered best knew where jobs were available. Her letter asked specific questions as to whether girls, who until now had been accustomed to milking cows, cleaning and undertaking common household work, would readily get places in the interior. She wanted to know what wages these girls would get, and how many of them would be required over the next two years. She questioned whether good servants, such as housemaids and cooks, were likely to be required, and what would be the wages for them if they were, and how many would be wanted. Further questions followed in the same vein with regard to married couples with small families; and could young single boys and girls, from seven to fourteen, be protected and found work? Would young women be able to save from their wages—were clothes as expensive as she had heard? And what would be the cheapest way of conveying people into the country?[51]

Caroline found many women work as domestic servants. The women could 'learn valuable social and domestic skills which might lead to a better marriage than she might otherwise expect'. It also gave the women an opportunity to earn their own livelihood and obtain a sense of freedom.[52]

Australian feminists in the 1960s and 1970s wondered if Caroline was 'a do-gooder but not really with it?'[53] Miriam Dixon, writing in 1976, was concerned with the inferior status of women in Australian culture, an inferiority stemming from attitudes that had evolved, she believed, from male convicts or colonial authorities with little self-esteem. To enable them to feel superior, such men treated women negatively. Dixon believed that the social status of women in Australia at that time was considerably lower than in other comparable countries.

In making her judgements, Dixon did not take into account the high esteem with which nineteenth-century contemporaries regarded unmarried women who were prepared to be frugal and industrious. John Capper's *Emigrant's Guide to Australia*, published in 1853, notes, for example, that drawing-room accomplishments were of no value, but the virtues of 'churning, baking, preserving, cheese-making, and similar matters' were highly prized.[54] Capper continues: 'such a helper [a wife] will not only be no expense, but she will actually often earn nearly as much as the husband'.[55] Mrs Clacy, writing of her visit to Australia in 1852–53, commented that the scarcity of women would prove an advantage to single women: 'the worst risk you run is getting married and finding yourself treated with twenty times the respect you may meet with in England. Here (as numbers go) women beat the "lords of creation"; in Australia it is the reverse, and there we may be pretty sure of having our own way'.[56] Mrs Clacy obviously did not feel that women were showing signs of low self-esteem.

Charles Dickens, with the financial help of Angela Burdett-Coutts, founded Urania Cottage, where prostitutes in London were rehabilitated and retrained and sent out to Australia as free settlers.[57] Neither Burdett-Coutts nor Dickens believed they were degrading the women. Caroline stated in a letter to the editor of the Melbourne *Argus* that, 'we ought not to forget that if this country is to become a great nation, we must endeavour to uphold in the females who come here principles of self-reliance and independence'.[58]

Caroline was concerned not only for the morals of the country but also that the females should be self-reliant and independent—not subservient. Dixon and her contemporaries did not take into account the circumstances of her day. She had no choice but to find work for the women as servants. There were few other opportunities for poor single females arriving in New South Wales. She did not see the work as degrading to the women; indeed, in her emigration lectures, she often used phrases that showed she felt the women were in control of the men, and that she did not see women solely as servants. In her lecture at Northampton in March 1853, for instance, she emphatically exclaimed, 'I never can imagine that Almighty God sent females into the world to be cooks and housemaids all their days'.[59] She did not see her work as 'stimulating' emigration, but as a 'simple object ... to provide for the comfort of the emigrant in a practical and respectable manner'. She 'observed the sufferings, the struggles, and the privations of thousands [in England]; and saw also the obstacles which lay between the sufferers here and the place where their condition might be improved'. This is the voice of a woman who genuinely believed she was helping women to find a better life in Australia. There was substance in her view. In 1977, R. Dalziel observed in his article in the *New Zealand Journal of History* that the patriarchal subordination of wife to husband did not appear to be a general characteristic of nineteenth-century pioneering societies. He believed that the working-class women leaving the slums of Britain gained from improved material circumstances, and middle-class women confronting a busy but purposeful and stimulating life often felt the colonies had offered them a fuller existence.[60]

Caroline soon found that the young women for whom she had found employment were afraid of travelling into the outback. To allay such fears, she led large parties of immigrants herself, drawing courage, no doubt, from her experience of travelling in India. She organised resting stages and employment agencies at a dozen rural centres—at Parramatta, Port Macquarie, Moreton Bay, Wollongong, Maitland, Scone, Liverpool, Campbelltown, Goulburn, Yass and Bong Bong.[61] To keep costs to a minimum, she advertised in the local papers requesting of farmers that she and her immigrants be allowed the use of empty bullock drays returning to farmsteads after bringing produce into Sydney. The farmers willingly supported her, and helped feed her and her immigrants, free of charge, on their journeys into the bush. Neither Caroline nor her immigrants were ever attacked by bushrangers; they seemed to admire the work she was undertaking.

The Immigrants' Home was expanded to include accommodation for families and young men, and housed the only free employment registry. Caroline, well ahead of her time, insisted that contracts of employment should be drawn up in triplicate—one for herself, one for the employee and one for the employer. The contracts were hardly ever contested.

Caroline's report, titled *Female Immigration, considered, in a Brief Account of the Sydney Immigrants' Home*, written after the first year's work, gives us an insight into her character. She admits, for instance, that she enjoys a challenge: 'I am such a lover of difficulties'.[62] We are able to see her sense of humour, her perseverance, her strengths and her frailties, and even her psychological approach, which came in use when trying to help the more lazy immigrants to find work. In fact, she suggested in her report that she would 'ask some humane and good people [she knew] not to give money' to those men she classified as 'Do-nothings' or 'Black-riband Gentry', for a good appetite would force them to work. The men were perfectly fit and able, but believed they should not have to work as hard in Australia as they had in Britain. Caroline 'felt a little triumph, in which, I fear, pride was mixed with thankfulness'. She was aware, however, that those feelings of pride were natural, but needed 'watching and regulating'.[63] She apologises for 'taking a pecuniary view', for she believed some in Australia would see it as an insult. Nonetheless she stated her views clearly and concisely and certainly did not pull her punches.

Her sarcasm comes across when she points out she had not received a reply to her letter written to the Governor. Hers was sent through the immigration office, and from there to the Colonial Secretary's Office, and then to the Governor. What reply was made by His Excellency, she was not able to say, for the answer was sent 'per *state coach, a remarkable slow conveyance*; but as the road from the colonial secretary's office to the domain-gate is now under repair, I may receive a favourable answer in time for the next arrival of immigrants'.[64]

Caroline observed how the mistreatment of servants often resulted in their reacting badly, and how this damaged not only the servants' prospects but also the reputation of the colony.[65]

In the report, she related how she was frightened by an experience with 'an old colonist, a man of experience, the father of a family' who commented that 'women were creatures of impulse and feeling; he admired their virtues, but deplored their want of judgment and stability'. He told her that she was doing wrong by 'sending souls to perdition! to send girls to the country [was] monstrous'. The old colonist berated her, threatening to give the Australian newspaper cuttings of all the murders and outrages of 'years past' to the English papers. As he spoke he walked up and down her office, his pacing becoming more and more hurried. She grew concerned and 'thought him mad, and quietly removed the penknife and ruler. I knew that even madmen will sometimes fall into the same pace as their keepers, I therefore joined him in his promenade, and he soon kept pace with me.' The old colonist later confessed that a convict had ruined his sister, and she had had a child and was in Sydney struggling to make ends meet. The man who had 'ruined' her had been sent to Van Diemen's Land; the colonist had been concerned with building his business and had treated his sister like a servant and 'he forgot his duty—hence her ruin'. Caroline ascertained the whereabouts of the sister and, together with the old colonist, went to visit her. She found that she still had feelings for the man and let 'nature … [do]

its work'. A happy reconciliation followed and the old colonist, at Caroline's suggestion, paid his sister's passage to Van Diemen's Land, arranged for her marriage and agreed to stock a farm for them. On visiting Caroline a few days later, he told her he had resolved 'never to cut out extracts from papers, or visit a philanthropist with money in his pocket'.[66]

Caroline very cleverly took advantage of the colonial newspapers to publicise her work, raise subscriptions, and obtain assistance in transporting immigrants into the bush, or for a hearse with which to bury the poor of Sydney.

Margaret Bolton, who had sailed on the ship *Carthaginian*, told Caroline of the horrors of her journey to Australia, particularly the brutal attack on herself. Margaret had been 'hauled from her bed in the middle of the night, doused with buckets of water, pinioned with her hands behind her back and left shivering in the poop for hours in her nightgown. The captain, the doctor and the captain's uncle, the third mate, had so terrorised the bounty passengers in steerage that not one man who witnessed the savagery dared raise a hand to stop it.'[67] Margaret Bolton had not mixed well with the other women on board ship and was particularly outspoken against the half-dozen or so 'ladies of the town' who 'sang, danced and drank with the captain and surgeon each night'.[68] There were other instances of ill-treatment throughout the journey. On hearing of the gross misconduct of the captain and surgeon, Caroline demanded of magistrates Innes and Brown, both members of the Emigration Board, that a warrant be issued against the two men. The magistrates declined. Undaunted, she petitioned Governor Gipps informing him she was ready to prosecute and willing to go to prison herself if necessary.[69] A successful prosecution would bring reforms. The prosecution was indeed successful and in April 1842, in Sydney's Supreme

Court, Judge William Burton sentenced Captain Robert Robertson and the surgeon, Richard William Nelson, to six months' gaol for the cruelty at sea to their passenger Margaret Bolton. They were also fined £50 each. The press was most indignant and felt the sentence should have been for twelve months, not six.[70]

On 14 November 1843 Caroline gave evidence before a Select Committee on Distressed Mechanics and Labourers.[71] During her evidence she outlined a scheme for settling families on the land with long leases. The land-owning members of the committee opposed her scheme. She was not daunted, and with the financial help of Captain Robert Towns and the proprietors of the Wollongong steamers, she put her own scheme into operation.[72] Only twenty-three, and not the fifty families she hoped for, settled on the land at Shell Harbour, near Wollongong. Later that year she reported that the scheme had had some failures, but also added 'the plan had succeeded remarkably well considering the many difficulties thrown in the way'.

Caroline gave further evidence before another Committee on Distressed Labourers in 1844.[73] At the committee's request she advertised for the unemployed to register with her in order that a true record of unemployment in Sydney could be calculated. She again questioned the validity of the government's land purchase regulations, but the committee did not heed her remarks. She did not attempt to settle other families on the land as she had at Shell Harbour; she had proved her point, but wanted to concentrate her efforts upon making further journeys into the bush to seek employment for newly arrived immigrants.

Archibald set sail from Madras on 5 January 1845. The ship, the *Coringa*, arrived in Sydney via Trincomalee and Hobart Town on 11

March.[74] During Archibald's time in India, Caroline had become a very well known woman in Australia. She felt the best help she could give those intending to emigrate was detailed information from those who had already settled in the colony. Archibald supported his wife by helping her gather evidence from the settled immigrants. Caroline and Archibald travelled throughout New South Wales, at their own expense, collecting over six hundred statements from immigrants about their lives in Australia. It was Caroline's hope that the British Government would publish these statements, but it declined to do so. It was whilst collecting these statements that Caroline was made aware of the large numbers of children who had been left behind in England and of the wives and children of ticket-of-leave men who had not been allowed free passage to Australia. Caroline was to publish some of the statements herself when she arrived back in England, and some of them were used by Charles Dickens in *Punch* magazine. The information acquired was also useful to Caroline when giving evidence to the various Select Committees.

On 4 September 1845 Caroline was called in by the committee set up by the Legislative Council of New South Wales to inquire into and report upon the best measure for promoting immigration.[75] She read a number of the statements that she and Archibald had collected 'from immigrants in various parts of the colony, relative to the improvement of their circumstances, caused by the emigrating to NSW'. It was during her evidence that Caroline raised the question of ticket-of-leave men being allowed to have their 'wives and families sent to the colony passage free', as she considered that 'the separation from their families' was a source of 'great evil'. She also put forward the suggestion that 'female immigrants should be sent out under the guardianship of respectable ladies' and made clear her disapproval of females coming out under what was called the protection of families.[76] She put forward the idea of ships with married families, preferring that no single men be sent out in the same ship as single women. She also stated categorically that she thought the system of bounty emigration was a 'very bad one, thoroughly bad'. Caroline could not propose a better system at that time, but stated that, once she had ascertained the actual demand for labour by visiting the districts and discussing with employers the question of country dispersion, she hoped to be able to submit a proposal to the Honourable Commissioners for Emigration. She then stated her belief that it was the 'poor peasantry that was wanted in the colony, settled upon small farms'.

In his book *Emigration and the Labouring Poor – Australian Recruitment in Britain and Ireland, 1831–1860* Robin Haines goes into great detail about the emigration schemes in operation. Appendix 4 details the agencies, regulations and the glossary of terms in operation between 1831 and 1900, and highlights the complexity of the emigration systems that Caroline had to come to terms with. Between 1840 and 1872 the Colonial Land and Emigration Commission (CLEC) selected and supervised emigration, including monitoring the bounty system until 1843 and taking control of it thereafter, until its cessation in the mid-1840s.[77]

Both the bounty and government schemes were in operation during the period 1837 to 1843, but it was the former system that was favoured. The bounty system was operated to Wakefield's principles of land sales and emigration—colonial land being sold to assist emigration. There were difficulties with the initial scheme, under which general 'permissions' to introduce emigrants were granted by the colonial authorities and payment was made for them in the colony on their safe arrival, fixed sums being laid down for various categories. Later on the system was altered, and tenders were invited for carrying out specified numbers of people at a certain rate per statute adult, this rate to be paid by the colony. The contractors were to be allowed to collect £1 from the emigrants themselves, but no further payment. Judgement on the fitness of the emigrants was passed by the colony on their arrival. It appears that this system did not work altogether satisfactorily and tended to introduce emigrants of an unsuitable type. One of the problems was that emigrants had to be maintained by the colonial government until they could get employment or whenever they became unemployed. Many decided that they would rather work on government projects at low wages than go as labourers to out-of-the-way farms. There was also the difficulty of fixing the 'sufficient price' of land at a rate that would prevent people from buying it before they were ready to develop it. The administration, which had been financed by means of loans raised on the security of future revenue, including land sales, was careless and extravagant and landed the colony in debt.[78]

Both schemes were open to abuse, but particularly the bounty system whereby representatives of approved ship-owners selected emigrants. Following the successful inspection of each emigrant by the Immigration Officer on arrival in the colony, the shipping company or its representative authorised to introduce emigrants claimed the bounty—a set rate between £18 and £19 for carrying each passenger. If the emigrant was rejected because of ill health, was deemed to be of poor character, considered the wrong age or to have an occupation not suitable to the colony, payment of the bounty was refused and the ship-owner was liable for the cost of transportation.[79] No payment was given if the emigrant died en route.

Government schemes were those of assisted, free or selected emigration. Initially, assisted passages were for those who did not qualify for a free passage as their occupation or age was incompatible with the needs of the colony. Assistance was calculated on a scale determined by occupation, gender, marital status and age. Assisted passages could be given, for instance, to aged relatives travelling with those who qualified for a free passage. From 1849 the assisted and free method of emigration was dispensed with and a new complex sliding scale of support introduced.[80]

A further scheme in operation during Caroline's time in New South Wales was the nominated system. This was the system whereby those who purchased land could nominate one to three labourers for each £100 of land purchased.[81]

Caroline did not comment on the relative merits between the bounty and government systems when writing *Female Immigration* in 1842. Her knowledge of the government system was only through hearsay, but she had been able to observe the 'evils' of the bounty system. She was incensed by the lack of protection given to young women that she 'solemnly avowed' was necessary. It was this, she believed, that caused the ruin of many young women.[82] The system also did not allow for the protection of the young women once they had arrived in Sydney, and Caroline voiced her concern that disreputable men and women were allowed on board ship shortly after its arrival to speak to and engage the women. In some instances Caroline felt the bounty agents were harshly treated when they were blamed for the poor character of the women they shipped to Australia, when in truth it was the lack of protection and assistance upon disembarkation that led to their ruination. Caroline was also concerned that the importers were allowed the liberty of selecting their own surgeon, whom she felt was often inadequately trained. She also felt that the examination of the emigrants on arrival in Sydney to assess the eligibility of payment of the bounty was not always carried out evenly, justly or correctly.[83]

By the 1850s squatters had acquired most of the land suitable for agricultural and pastoral purposes. In September 1826 Governor Darling established an area known as the Limits of Location. Settlers were permitted to take up land within this area, but not beyond its boundaries. Land outside the limits was not sold or let. In 1829 Darling issued a second order extending the original boundaries to establish what became known as the Nineteen Counties surrounding Sydney.[84] Settlement within these new areas was permitted, but again no land could be acquired or occupied beyond the Nineteen Counties. During the 1830s many ex-convicts as well as some emigrants illegally occupied land outside the boundaries. In some instances they also stole stock to put onto the land on which they were squatting. The colonial government did not have the power or the resources to remove them from Crown land. In 1833 Governor Bourke took action to ensure the squatters could not claim legal title and in 1836 imposed an annual licence fee of £10. This gave the squatters grazing rights, but also ensured that the Crown kept the title to the land. The squatters, wool manufacturers and importers to Britain wielded considerable power, socially, economically and politically both in Britain and Australia. It was in the early 1840s that home government fixed a minimum price of £1 per acre for land within the Nineteen Counties. Land outside the area, particularly unsurveyed land, was not available. This made it impossible to obtain fertile land until the authorities put it up for sale. Even when they did put land on the open market there was often insider trading adding to the problems of the poor acquiring small plots of land. The squatters gained security of tenure and pre-emptive rights in 1847. This had the effect of locking up the land and making it impossible for the emigrant, or emancipist, to purchase land for fourteen years. There was much land grabbing and under-occupation by the squatters. Some even left managers in charge of the land and returned to live in Britain.

During her seven years in New South Wales Caroline was able to come to terms with and appreciate the problems that the regulations raised and was able to make her own judgement on the systems in operation. Such was her ability and understanding of the situation that Mr Hanson, when he proposed a vote of thanks to Mrs Chisholm following her lecture on 'Free Selection before Survey' in Sydney on 10 December 1860, remarked, 'no one had worked so hard as Mrs Chisholm in the cause of the people, and had received so little for it. She knew more than many of their statesmen about the land question.'[85]

As Caroline prepared to depart for England in April 1846, the Scottish Presbyterian Minister John Dunmore Lang, who was also involved in the field of emigration, was preparing to sail to England as well. Before his departure he published a letter in the local paper, openly accusing Caroline as being a 'zealous and devoted Roman Catholic' who was trying to romanise the colony.[86] This was just one of a number of attacks John Dunmore Lang was to make upon Caroline's work. Though hurt by his attacks, she was more than able to defend herself. Caroline's reply to Lang shows her devotion to her faith and the contribution of her work:

> It has been acknowledged that I have done some good to the colony, favoured neither country nor creed, and in truth, charity knows no

> such distinction—asks not to what nation or religious profession the object of her compassion belongs—this is my principle and part of my creed,—'the good of the whole', is my pledge ... To do good is often weary work; to watch our motives, and to endeavour to keep them pure and holy is a struggle—a constant warfare with human nature;—to act on the Samaritan principle requires the grace of God; conscious of my own weakness, anxious to do good to all men, am I not to be allowed to address my Maker after a weary day's work in the way that my conscience dictates; I dearly love justice and the praise of men may be pleasant to me; but a consciousness of my own integrity is more so; for when I lose the approbation of my own mind, I forfeit one of the sweetest comforts that God permits a human being to enjoy.[87]

Dr John Dunmore Lang had originally arrived in Sydney with his parents in 1824 but returned to England to obtain his Doctorate of Divinity with an annual stipend of £30. He returned to Australia around 1826 (twelve years before Caroline and her family). Lang commuted between England and Australia promoting both educational institutions and emigration. He firmly believed, as did Caroline, that the grinding poverty of Britain could readily be relieved for some by the boundless opportunities in Australia.[88] He believed the Roman Catholic Church was making every effort 'not only to rivet the chains of popery on a deluded people in the Australian Colonies, but to extend the reign of superstition over the neighbouring and highly interesting isles of the Pacific'.[89] Unsurprisingly, Lang favoured Presbyterians or Lutheran missionaries or German lay assistants as emigrants.

This was not the first occasion that Lang had commented upon the Roman Catholic Church, and particularly Irish Catholics in New South

Wales. He noted that no less than one-third of the total population of the colony in 1837 was composed of Irish Roman Catholics, of whom nineteen out of twenty were convicts or emancipated convicts.[90] In *The Question of Questions*, published in 1841 after his fifth voyage to England, Lang attacked the bounty system but also talked of his fear that the colony would be transformed into a 'Province of Popedom'. He wrote:

> posterity would declare that in the year 1838, His Excellency, Sir George Gipps, and his two Councils found NSW a thoroughly Protestant Colony; but that in the short space of three years thereafter, they had done more to transform it into a mere Province of Popedom, a mere receptacle for the worst portion of the population of Europe than had been done by all the injudicious acts of all his predecessors for fifty years before.[91]

The Irish faced a harsh economic existence, especially during periods of potato famines and particularly during the Great Hunger. R. B. Madgwick, in his book *Immigration into Eastern Australia 1788–1851*, compiled statistics of assisted immigration to NSW between 1839 and 1851 that indicate that forty-eight per cent of the total 78,415 immigrants were from Ireland.[92]

Once back in England Lang again attacked Caroline's work in articles in the *British Banner*, which had a circulation chiefly among the more extreme Protestants. The articles began in March 1848 and did not cease until Lang again left England in November 1849. Lang wrote a particularly harsh article on board the *Clifton* while she lay off Gravesend before sailing to Australia which was published in the *British Banner* on 21 November 1849. Lang's main concern was to attack Earl Grey and the

Colonial Office for their neglect and discouragement of his schemes. From the spring of 1848, Grey allowed the emigration of Irish orphan girls from the workhouses to Australia. Lang thought it a measure 'to supply Roman Catholic wives for the English and Scottish Protestants of the humbler classes'. The article went on to suggest that these 'mixed marriages' were engineered by an 'artful female Jesuit, the able but concealed agent of the Romish priesthood in Australia, who had thus adroitly managed to attach both your lordships … to her apron strings'.[93]

Lang's opposition to Caroline was no doubt because of her Catholicism, but perhaps also because of jealousy and hurt pride that a Roman Catholic, and a woman, who had only been working in the field of emigration for seven years was more popular than himself. There had been a proposal to present Mrs Chisholm with a testimonial and gift before she left Australia. Dr Lang subscribed to the testimonial, but one can imagine that his contribution was made with mixed feeling. Lang had been anxious to become a paid accredited agent/watchdog putting forward Australia's interests in England, but his wish was denied.

During her seven years in Australia, Caroline achieved a great deal. In that short time she had become so well respected that the Legislative Council had requested her to give evidence before them on three separate occasions. It must have been a disappointment that the council did not accept her ideas or that arrangements had not been made for the better reception of immigrants (reforms were made a few years after Caroline's return to England). The Sydney Female Emigrants' Home placed 735 young women in employment with wages varying from £10 to £18 a year; 291 of those young women were found employment in country districts. There were 394 Roman Catholics, 238 Protestants of the Established Church, and 103 Presbyterians. In total there were 516 Irish young women, 184 English and thirty-five Scottish girls. Caroline proudly stated that she had received £156 in subscriptions, paid out £154, had £2 in cash and was expecting a further £11 in subscriptions. There were no debts.[94] In all, Caroline had placed nearly 11,000[95] immigrants in employment, and was, as she herself believed, 'the first lady in Australia who had ventured in the character of an author, to appear before the public'.[96]

Caroline achieved all this, yet for the majority of the time she was without the help and support of her husband who was serving overseas in India. The fears for the health of the family, who could so easily have caught diseases from newly arrived emigrants at the Immigration Barracks, and the wide scope of her work, meant that Caroline was deprived of the company of the children, who were cared for by the Nanny, Miss Galvin, at the family home in Windsor.

Caroline showed remarkable patience and determination in pursuing her aims of establishing the home when faced with the opposition of not only the Governor of NSW, but also both the Protestant and Catholic clergy. She showed that she was not afraid to lead large parties of immigrants into the bush. All this was achieved without a penny being paid out by the Colonial Government. Caroline would not accept financial assistance, believing that to do so would jeopardise her independence to 'serve all creeds' to the best of her ability. Monies were raised by subscription, and help sought from 'hospitable settlers' in helping to transport the emigrants into the interior and to provide food and shelter along the way. In evidence to the House of Lords, Caroline acknowledged that she had lent 'some hundred pounds in small sums to the labouring poor' while conducting the emigration home in Sydney. However she only lost a total of £16. The rest of the sums had been repaid.[97]

Caroline's departure enabled the people of Sydney to demonstrate the regard in which she was held. The Committee of the Legislative Council of New South Wales recorded 'their grateful sense of the valuable services of a lady to whose benevolent exertions … this colony is under the highest obligations'. Robert Lowe who spoke at the Council Meeting said, 'One person only, in the colony has done anything effectual—anything on a scale which may be called large—to mitigate this crying evil and national sin, and to fix families on our lands in lieu of bachelors. And, strange to say, that one is a humble, unpretending, quiet-working female missionary! An emigrant missionary!—not a clerical one!'[98]

Eight members of the Legislative Council, together with principal magistrates and landowners, were appointed to a Testimonial Committee, without distinction of religion or politics, to raise funds for Mrs Chisholm, and subsequently raised a subscription of £150. They gave an address which:

> thanked Mrs Chisholm for her zealous exertions on behalf of the emigrant population and … the extraordinary efforts which you have made have been dictated by a spirit of most enlightened benevolence. In the establishment of an emigrants' home, in procuring the advantageous settlement of great numbers of the emigrant population in the interior as servants and occupants of small farms, in the large collection of statistical facts and voluntary information derived from the labouring classes, your exertions have proved of singular benefit to the community.[99]

Sir George Gipps added his testimony to the many tributes to Caroline. He stated: 'I cannot give a stronger evidence of the economy of people working for themselves, than by referring to what has been done by Mrs Chisholm; and I am glad of this opportunity of doing justice to that lady's exertions, and do it with much greater pleasure and satisfaction, from having at the commencement of her labours thrown cold water upon her plans.'

Caroline accepted the testimonial 'to expend it in further promoting emigration, by restoring wives to their husbands, and children to their parents', and added 'it is my intention if supported by your co-operation, to attempt more than I have hitherto performed'.[100]

Meeting of Family Colonisation Loan Society at the British Institution, Tabernacle Row, City Road, London, addressed by Lord Shaftesbury. *Illustrated London News*, 28 February 1852.

Chisholm home in Islington

Bust of Caroline Chisholm given to her by Pope Pius IX.
By kind permission of Don Chisholm.

ENGLAND AND EMIGRATION 1846–1854

Caroline and Archibald sailed back to England on the *Dublin* with Archibald junior, William and Henry, aged ten, nine and seven. As the ship neared its destination after nearly four months at sea, Caroline gave birth to her fourth son, Sydney, on 6 August 1846. She was unable to feed the baby. Provisions were low and there was only one goat left on board; the passengers fed it with ship's biscuits and ensured that milk was saved for the child. On arrival in Hull, the disembarking passengers decorated the goat with ribbons and led it in procession with Caroline and baby Sydney.[1]

While recovering from the birth and settling herself and Archibald and the four boys in London, Caroline started her campaign for a better system of emigration to the Australian colonies. On 25 January 1847, she sent a letter to Earl Grey, the Secretary of State for the Colonies, from 20 Prince's Street, Jubilee Place, Mile End. Caroline introduced herself saying that 'it may not be unknown to your Lordship that I interested myself for a period of eight years in NSW in trying to ameliorate the condition of Emigrants on their arrival there, and other classes of the community who wanted employment'. She mentioned that his predecessor had tendered his thanks for the services she had rendered to emigrants, and said she felt that the experience she had gained enabled her to write to his Lordship on the subject of Emigration 'and on the evils that press so heavily upon the social and moral advancement of that colony'.

Caroline drew Grey's attention to the 'numerous and daily applications' which she received from 'country labourers and whole families for a free passage to NSW and Port Phillip', particularly from the relatives of those who had emigrated to Australia, the majority Irish. She said that she had received three hundred applications on one day, and felt it lamentable that the 'earnest solicitations of these poor people for a free passage to NSW' were not met when she knew of the 'vast and suitable field which New Holland offers for the enterprising and industrious emigrant'.

Caroline mentioned the large disparity of the sexes in the colony, 'men being out of all proportion in number to women', and from this 'flows misery and crime, I dare not dwell upon'. She went on to observe that 'this unnatural anomaly of the human race' was the cause 'in a great degree, [of] the gradual but certain extermination of those unfortunate tribes, the Aborigines of New Holland' who, as 'the original holders of the soil, demand the speedy and parental interference of a humane government'. With the hope of 'removing to some extent this crying and national evil', she begged 'most respectfully to say that I would feel disposed to co-operate in finding a remedy by making a selection of young women of good character as free emigrants to Australia'.

Caroline went on 'deferentially to remark that the present policy of sending women under penal sentence to NSW' only added 'infinitely to the moral evil'. She stated that she had 'never met but with one man who did not express extreme desire to be married to a woman of good character'. She added that it was an erroneous opinion that women sent under the penal sentence 'make suitable wives enough for reclaimed convict men', and further that, 'nature and moral religion both shrink from the idea of such characters as mothers of children'. The reformed prisoner received back into the social order of society was 'sensitive upon that point'. Caroline had met the unfortunate emancipist living alone, and at times had found 'two young men associated together because they could not meet with respectable females to whom they could offer otherwise a comfortable home'. She was also aware that 'respectable emigrant parents object to their daughters serving in the same establishment' with women who had been sent out under penal sentence.

Caroline concluded her letter by remarking it would be easy to place 'young women, as may be disposed to emigrate, soon after their arrival' with 'respectable families in Australia, and by the yeomen of the country'. 'More particularly' she felt that 'the demand for servants in the interior is on the increase'. She was concerned that the young women should be protected on their passage out, as well as on their arrival in the colony and after dispersion in the interior. The subject was of such 'paramount importance to their welfare', it would afford her 'deep and sincere satisfaction to impart that information and knowledge which I have gained relative thereto from experience'.

Caroline's letter was referred to the Land and Emigration Commissioners, with the suggestion that she contact them. Earl Grey desired that 'his sincere thanks' be conveyed to her, and that 'he entertains of the value of … [her] observations, and of the spirit of benevolence' expressed in her communication.

What this letter and the reply show is Caroline's clear grasp of the problems and her practical solution to them.

Caroline remembered the promise she made to the settled emigrants when she and Archibald collected their statements in New South Wales before her departure. She remembered the emancipists who were desperate to have their wives and families sent out to the colony, and the anxious parents who had been unable to take their children with them to Australia. The children had been left behind in England because they were either too young or too ill to travel, or the parents lacked the funds.

It was as a result of Caroline's determined efforts in locating, documenting and detailing the whereabouts of the children that the ship the *Sir Edward Parry* was chartered to take the children to their families in Australia. The Colonial Land and Emigration Commission report for 1847 noted their concern that '211 applications' had been received 'on behalf of children, of whom 161 are under 14 years of age, and of whom 205 are living in Ireland, and are scattered over 20 counties'. The commission admitted 'frankly ... we should not ourselves have ventured to suggest a large juvenile emigration, but, being anxious to meet the wishes expressed by the Colonial Government [instigated by Caroline] ... no effort shall be wanting on our part to fulfil successfully the benevolent designs in which it originated'.[2]

With the blessing of the commission Caroline and Archibald contacted the children, negotiated details with the foster parents, and arranged clothing for the trip and collection and transportation to Plymouth for embarkation. The ship arrived safely in Sydney on 17 February 1848. The agent's list completed on arrival gives an indication of the problems Archibald and Caroline must have faced.[3] There were thirty-three Irish youngsters up to the age of fourteen on board, and two from England; and thirty-nine Irish children over the age of fourteen, with three from England and two from Scotland. The Irish youngsters came from most of the counties of Ireland, the English youngsters from Cambridgeshire and Middlesex and the Scots from Fifeshire. There were also five couples—three from Ireland and two from England—with seven children. The majority of the passengers could read and write: twenty-three could read but not write and only thirteen were unable to do either.

The departure of the *Sir Edward Parry* did not go unnoticed: a report appeared in Douglas Jerrold's *Weekly Newspaper* of 23 October 1847.[4] The correspondent noted that the colonial government had been led by the appeals of Mrs Chisholm, and quoted *The Australian*: 'Mrs Chisholm is a woman whose advice on any subject within her sphere would be worth attending to; for she has a public political mind, singularly practical and judicious'.

While tracing the children, Caroline also discussed with the home government the plight of emancipists' wives and families, whom she believed should be sent to join their partners in the colony free of charge. When the system of transportation had been at its height, the home government had allowed a grant of a free passage to Australia for the wives and children of those convicts who had served their term of imprisonment. (This imprisonment, however, was not incarceration. Prisoners were assigned duties as labourers and servants, or worked on government buildings.) Due to economic pressures, however, free passage for wives and children had been discontinued in 1842, causing hardship to many of the emancipists in Australia and their families in Britain. But in April 1847, through Caroline's efforts, a number of wives and families sailed for Australia, free of charge, to join their partners. Caroline had accumulated all the information and data concerning the children and wives and families. As a writer suggests in 1862, 'it is one of the characteristics of

Caroline Chisholm, that she never makes a claim or a charge—whether it be against a government department or a commercial system—which she is not prepared to establish with the strongest judicial proof'.[5]

Caroline was called as a witness before the select committee of the House of Lords enquiring into the execution of criminal law on 20 April 1847.[6] The knowledge she had gained of the rules of 'convict discipline' would have made her an excellent witness. She was asked 'if she had heard many say that they found Transportation to be a less punishment than they thought it to be previously to coming out'. She said that she had 'frequently' heard people say so. During the course of her evidence she stated that she had placed about one thousand 'ticket of leave' men in employment in New South Wales and a number of emancipists in jobs in the interior, because the men themselves had felt that 'Sydney was a place of danger, where they would be exposed to great temptation'. She went on to explain that the success of ex-convicts depended largely on their getting away from their old associates. She explained that she had 'knowledge of character in the selection of masters' that enabled her to place them with good masters where she knew they would not be taunted for being ex-convicts.[7]

During the summer of 1847 Caroline published *Emigration and Transportation Relatively Considered*, a booklet cum open letter dedicated, by permission, to The Right Honourable Earl Grey. The purpose of the letter was to persuade the government to follow a systematic plan of emigration. Caroline starts with an apology: 'if the subject which I am desirous of advocating be not of sufficient importance to plead my apology for thus addressing you, there is nothing which I could say that would make the act excusable'.[8] She then spells out her plans 'with the sound spirit of political economy.'[9] Appended are eighteen statements of 'voluntary information of the people of NSW, collected by Mrs Chisholm'. For Caroline it was:

> common sense to solve the financial question, as to whether it is better to endeavour to support the overburdened labour market of the United Kingdom by the instrumentality of Government works which are not required, and by an augmentation of the poor rates; or whether it would not be more in accordance with the sound spirit of political economy to give a free passage to her Majesty's Colonies, to such eligible families as should voluntarily come forward and solicit this boon.[10]

She felt it far better that the poor, 'instead of being as they are now, an encumbrance to the State', should be enabled to emigrate and thus 'become an industrious population ... [that] would contribute to the commercial revenue of Great Britain annually'.[11]

In *Emigration and Transportation*, Caroline also raised the issue of the land question. She could see the absurdity that there was a constant cry of 'no funds' to give free passage to the Australian Colonies when 'if land be not put up for sale, land cannot be sold; consequently there are no funds'. She noted that when:

> land was required by the large capitalists, or men merely land jobbers, land was put up for sale, and funds were raised; aye, even when it was known that gambling was being carried on to a frightful extent, land was put up and sold, when men bought on chance with accommodation paper.[12]

Her practical solution was to 'temper the supply' of labour 'to the demand' for it, by means of assisted emigration:

> Labour, it may be seen, will create capital; that capital will bring out emigrants, and find employment for them; thus a self-creating and a co-operating system would, in a shorter time than is calculated upon, provide for hundreds of thousands. The late consumer in Europe now becomes a producer in Australia; he finds a remunerative return for his labour; he transforms it into capital, and that capital enables him in his turn to employ labour.[13]

This was not the first time Caroline had raised the land question, nor was it the last. She touched on the subject during all four of her political lectures in Sydney during the late 1850s and early 1860s. The report of Caroline's lecture in Sydney on 10 December 1860 noted that:

> for some years the subject of a free selection of the land by the people, and for themselves, had been one which had occupied her mind, and fully was she persuaded of the fact of its being a subject of the deepest importance, and one which nearly affected the interest of every man, woman, and child of the community. She had made the land question in this colony a matter of deep study.[14]

The language and style of *Emigration and Transportation* suggests that it was the work of the 'writer' that Caroline had been 'obliged to engage'. She explained that 'The applications for information on various subjects connected with NSW are increasing every day' and 'the numerous letters we have received have occupied nearly the whole of my time and the best part of Captain Chisholm's to answer'.[15] Not only was the volume of letters becoming difficult to cope with, but she was not in the best of health. In a letter to Benjamin Hawes at the Colonial Office dated 28 February 1847, she mentions that 'indisposition' had prevented her making an early reply to his letter of the twelfth. While Caroline may have felt it necessary to raise her tone when addressing Earl Grey, such phrasing as 'in the spirit of captiousness', 'I intensely feel the solemnity and the responsibility of the question' and 'I hesitate not to say, iniquitously tried to depreciate and thwart the decrees of Providence in the propagation of the human race' is far removed from her simple and natural style of writing.

The response to Caroline's open letter and her repeated visits to the Colonial Office was not what she had hoped for. She failed to interest the government in her land-ticket system and family emigration. She was not to be defeated, however, and in 1849 she founded the Family Colonisation Loan Society. The society encouraged and helped families to accumulate the cost of half their fare, the remainder to be loaned by the society and to be repaid within two years in Australia. The Chisholm home at 3 Charlton Crescent in Islington, London became the Australian information centre, and letters addressed to 'Caroline Chisholm, London' actually reached her here. A letter addressed to 'Caroline Chisholm, Colonial Secretary's Office, Downing Street, London' was redirected to her home.[16] Interestingly, this letter was from a James Charles Kiernam who wrote from Battery Point, Hobart Town, on 25 February 1850, requesting Caroline's help and influence in obtaining a pardon from 'an unmerited and cruel sentence of Transportation'. This was not the first occasion he had written to her. As the letter was found in the archives of Sir Sidney Herbert, Caroline must have passed it on to him in order that he might look into the matter and advise.[17]

Following the publication of *Emigration and Transportation*, Caroline gave evidence before the select committee of the House of Lords on Colonisation from Ireland on 12 July 1847. She was cross-examined on her work in Sydney, transporting single females and groups of families into the bush to seek employment. The committee questioned her on her views on the fixed price of land at one pound per acre. She was not shy in stating that if 'the upset price were much lower numbers would buy land in large blocks, and that the people that want to get it would not, because they prefer selling land in large in preference to small quantities.'[18]

Caroline made good use of the statements she and Archibald had collected, but was concerned that their 'means will only allow me to print on a very limited scale', even though 'those who have had experience consider it desirable that the statements should be widely circulated, given away in every direction'. Mr Elliot of the Commissioners of Crown Lands and Emigration had indicated that he thought that the publication of Caroline's statements would cause quite a commotion in favour of emigration to the colony.[19] Some of the accounts of life in Australia were later published as *Comfort for the Poor! Meat Three Times a Day!!*

In August 1850 Caroline published a series of letters to 'the gentlemen forming the Committee of the Family Colonization Loan Society'. Entitled *The A.B.C. of Colonization*, the paper explains more fully the 'principle of the Society' and how it may 'be worked in detail in the Australian Colonies'.[20] As with *Emigration and Transportation*, the language and style of *The A.B.C. of Colonization* would seem to suggest that either Archibald or the 'writer' helped Caroline with its composition.

Caroline voiced her deep concern that 'orphan after orphan had been victimized on board emigrant ships'.[21] It is therefore no surprise that she was one of the founders of the British Ladies Female Emigrant Society (also known as The British Female Emigration Society: The British Matron Society) founded in March 1849. The society was not involved in promoting emigration, but was specifically established to find 'matrons' to escort single female emigrants to the colonies. Caroline strongly believed that time on board ship should be put to the best possible use. It was one of the aims of the society that matrons should be employed not only to protect the young single females from the attentions of sailors and single men, but also to ensure that they occupied their time usefully. The matrons encouraged them to make garments to be sold on arrival in Sydney and to learn to read and write if they could not already do so.[22]

Caroline often held regular evening meetings for prospective emigrants at the family home at 3 Charlton Crescent, where one of the rooms had been furnished as steerage accommodation. Sir Sidney Herbert often attended these meetings, as did Lord Shaftesbury, who was also on the society's committee. Caroline advised and helped families, suggesting ways in which they might combine to pool their resources so as to save two-thirds of the fare and money for clothing for the journey and equipment needed in the colony. She also ensured that single females would meet and join family groups to afford them protection on board ship and on arrival in Australia.

A form entitled 'Protection for Emigrants' was issued to each group. It asked that each person in the group enquire into the respectability of the other members. Once satisfied and happy with the people in the 'mess' they each had to sign the form to indicate that they 'voluntarily agreed to mess together during our voyage to Australia, and to afford parental protection to such young persons as are admitted into our Group, and will consider and treat them as members of our family'. A member of the group was to be elected to communicate directly with her and pass on information to the group. It was expected that the group would get to know one another before departure.

The form listed all those in the group and the weekly supply of provisions. According to the society's Dietary Table every emigrant was entitled to draw sixteen weeks' rations. Scales, weights and measures were put on board. To prevent waste, parties who did not draw the quantity to which they were entitled from the weekly allowance could receive the quantity due to them on leaving the ship. It was felt the reserve would be useful to the emigrant if they went up country, or until they had permanent employment. In case the voyage was longer than expected, the society put on board water and provisions for twenty-two weeks. To ensure that the messes had all their entitlement, the groups were provided with printed receipts for their weekly rations. Printed receipts were also issued for any necessary medical comforts. The captain was required to deliver the receipts of the emigrants, or the provisions, to the society's agent in the colony on arrival.[23] Caroline's requirement that the captain provide proof that the emigrants had received the allotted provisions was no doubt a reaction to her experience and knowledge of the ill-treatment of passengers by ships' captains and surgeons.

Only when Caroline had resolved all the problems of her scheme did she approach the men she wished to be on her committee.[24] That she appointed Lord Shaftesbury to head the society was an act of inspiration and she dedicated an open letter to him in August 1849.[25] Shaftesbury was no mere figurehead, and was present at the public meetings organised by the Society.[26]

Lord Shaftesbury was acknowledged during his own lifetime as a leading parliamentarian, social reformer, and an ardent Church of

England evangelical. He was elected to parliament as a Tory in 1826. He was involved with industrial reforms, particularly the ten-hour movement that tried to restrict the hours young children worked in the mills in the north of England. He campaigned for improved working conditions for chimney sweeps and women and children working in the mines, for sanitary reforms, and for improvements in urban boarding houses. He was president of the Ragged School Union from 1846 until his death. The Union considered emigration an essential element of their overall plan.

Shaftesbury had voted against the Catholic Emancipation Act 1829 but was later to record his vote for emancipation as a member of the Commons and of the Government.[27] His own strong evangelical beliefs made him an excellent foil against those who accused Caroline of 'romanising' Australia. It was known that his 'bigoted fellow Protestants' did not approve of his co-operation with a Roman Catholic woman.[28] The Right Hon. Vernon Smith MP, speaking at a 'Testimonial to Mrs Chisholm' held at the London Tavern on Tuesday 9 August 1853, remarked:

> there was no possible motive for her exertions, but humanity and benevolence. She was a Roman Catholic and some opposition had been excited against her in this respect from the idea that her object was conversion.

He added:

> The best answer to this objection was that he and the Earl of Shaftesbury belonged to the Society, and he believed that nobody would accuse that noble Earl of taking any steps to favour of the Roman Catholic religion.[29]

There can be no doubt that Caroline admired Shaftesbury. Of her last political lecture in Sydney in June 1861 entitled 'Our Home Life' the *Empire* noted:

> She had been asked in Melbourne to give an evening to 'the education of the poor'. She replied that she would rather give a lecture on the education of the rich. It was the rich who needed education (laughter and cheers) not mere book learning, but such training as the Earl of Shaftesbury, the Honourable Mr Herbert and Lord Grosvenor could give them, acquired by observation of men. When she expressed her opinion on the subject, the Earl of Shaftesbury said 'Mrs Chisholm is right', and added that he would bring six mechanics meanly dressed, but in intellect and knowledge of the world superior to six gentlemen (Cheers).[30]

Caroline also supported the early closing movement in Australia and was concerned with the provision of housing for the poor in Sydney.

Shaftesbury's support for the ten-hour bill, his campaign for low-cost working-class accommodation, his interest in the Ragged Schools Union and the education of destitute children squared with her own campaign. That he admired her is not in doubt. *The Times*, reporting on a public meeting of emigrants about to proceed to Australia on the *Athenian*, a ship chartered by the society, noted Shaftesbury's closing comments:

> The audience had probably heard something of 'Bloomarism' which meant that ladies were to walk about in man's attire. (A laugh). Mrs Chisholm had attained the highest order of Bloomerism; she had the heart of a woman, and the understanding of a man. (Cheers). He wished

her 'God speed' and prayed that she might be made more and more instrumental in carrying out great and beneficent and holy purposes. (Loud cries of 'Hear, hear').[31]

At a society meeting held at the Royal British Institution in Tabernacle Row, City Road, London, on Wednesday, 18 February 1852, Shaftesbury concluded the meeting with a high eulogy of the talents and self-denial of Mrs Chisholm, saying 'The children shall rise up and call her blessed'.[32]

The appointment of Shaftesbury to chair the committee of the society did not silence all opposition to Caroline's choice of faith. She was often accused of 'romanising' Australia, yet the Canterbury Committee that quite openly recruited emigrants on a sectarian basis received no rebuke. It is not surprising that on 20 August 1850 Caroline wrote a very angry letter to Sir Sidney Herbert advising him that the Canterbury Committee had called upon her to revise the 'Test Act' and requested that she find emigrants on a sectarian basis to fill their ships.

The Canterbury Committee was formed in light of Edward Gibbon Wakefield's plans for a new colony in New Zealand. Wakefield was not 'noted for his piety' and although 'traditionally at odds with most members of the establishment he … courted them with a blueprint for an exclusively Church of England, Tory settlement in Canterbury [NZ] complete with a Bishop'. Wakefield also pleaded for 'new sectarian colonies "with the strong attraction for superior emigrants of a particular creed in each colony"'.[33] The government sanctioned the Canterbury Association and the Archbishop of Canterbury accepted its presidency. The committee comprised eighteen 'prominent clerics, sixteen aristocrats and eleven members of Parliament, including Archbishop Whately of Dublin, Bishop

Blomfield of London, Lord Ashley (Shaftesbury's earlier title), Sidney Herbert, the Earl of Lincoln and Lord John Manners'.

In her letter to Sir Sidney Herbert, Caroline was adamant that she would 'work for no sect, or party, the good of the whole is my object'. Caroline told the Canterbury Committee that she had 'long since refused to work with the Catholic Society and … could not work with theirs if a sectarian selection was to be made'. The committee had told Caroline that they had 'money and influence', but she told Sir Sidney that they did not have 'the influence that weighs with honest John Bull in his *working class*—they are in fact at a stand still for common Emigrants, they have expended £400 in circulars to the Clergy, who have done all they could but they cannot move the class they want'. The Canterbury Committee offered to take a party from the society 'just as they now stand on our books—to make no stiff enquiry'. Caroline continued, 'I really believe we have more good members of their church on the books of the Loan Society than they have themselves'. The move pleased Caroline, for she felt it 'desirable to extend the true principles of Colonisation and the more Colonies the Society aids the better, and a great blessing it is to see the true Samaritan principle of charity work its way, poor as we are we are rich, because we try to follow the command of one who drew no sectarian line'. Caroline felt it of great importance to get the society's first ship off, for then she could make up a party for the Canterbury Committee, if Sir Sidney felt it prudent. She could see no objection provided the Canterbury Committee selected people according to the *FCLS* rules.[34]

The *Slains Castle* was the first society ship. It sailed from London to Port Adelaide and Port Phillip on 28 September 1850, stopping at Gravesend on 30 September, arriving in Australia at the end of January 1851. The 700-ton barque[35] was under the command of Mr H. Andrews with a complement of crew of chief and second officer, Mr Phelps and Mr Malone; a surgeon, Mr McCaul; twelve able seaman, four apprentices, a ship's carpenter, a steward, one cuddy servant and two cooks.[36] The society despatched about two hundred and fifty men, women and children, of whom 'one hundred and twenty communicants were Church of England, two Jewesses, and others equally divided between Wesleyans and Roman Catholics', highlighting the non-sectarian selection of passengers.[37] The emigrants had paid by instalments some £1,403 towards the cost of their passage, and the society lent £865 to be repaid in two years by earnings in the colony. When Eneas Mackenzie wrote his *Memoirs* in 1852 he noted that part of the loan had already been repaid.

The ship was anchored at East India Export Dock before departure and attracted a large number of friends and relatives of those about to depart for Australia, as well as those just curious to view the boat before she sailed. Mackenzie remarked that all those who visited the ship were 'highly gratified with the arrangements and contrast afforded to other vessels engaged in the same service'.

The arrangements on board differed from earlier emigrant ships, in that Caroline arranged separate cabins, and the society's vessels gave ten per cent more space to the emigrant than was compulsory under the Passenger Act.[38] Mackenzie noted that those cabins 'intended for a man and his wife were of a certain size, while those for a party of females were larger'. He continued:

> The bedsteads for a married couple consisted of broad stout laths, one-half of the length of which were placed to fit into the other, so that when not needed to sleep upon they could be slid back, and the bedstead

become one half the size. By this contrivance there was a couch formed for the day, and by a broad sliding in a support for the back, while the room gained left a private cabin for the occupants. A wash stand in a corner, and some other trifling articles, completed the fittings. In some of these there was a small bed-place a little above for a young child. In the young women's cabins two sides had each two berths, while another side had a couch which drew out to allow a mother and daughter, or elderly female and young child, to sleep upon. This last-named party had charge of the young women in the cabin; and, as one of the girls in the group was selected from having parents on board, her mother had a right to entry to see her daughter; thus a double guardianship become exercised. By a space being left at the bottom, and the frame-work not reaching the roof by several inches, a free and perfect circulation of air was allowed in each cabin, besides, there being a small window covered by a piece of coloured cotton; thus there were privacy, air and light. At the end of this deck were domestic offices for females and children while others for men were on deck. At the bows a part was partitioned off for the young men, where there were two ranges of bed places, and tables, with ample room, where in quiet and retirement they could pursue their studies during the voyage. Down the centre of the deck between the cabins were tables for the meals and other purposes of the emigrants, above which were shelving for the dishes.

The completeness and excellence of the arrangements are thus seen, while, the passengers having the use of the entire deck and poop of the vessel, it must be acknowledged that every means was taken to render them comfortable and healthy; their interest being considered paramount in every particular.[39]

Before the second ship set sail the society faced a dilemma. It was felt necessary to appoint a colonial agent, but the society lacked the funds required. Caroline and Archibald made a painful decision: Archibald would go out to Australia and act gratuitously as the agent. It would not be easy to cope with a further separation which would stretch their already meagre funds. They were recovering from the death of Sarah who was born in February 1850 but died six months later from a throat infection. Caroline had fallen pregnant again and the baby was due in late July 1851. There was also Caroline Monica, born 13 May 1848, to consider. In March 1851, Archibald sailed for Australia at his own expense on the *King William*, arriving in Adelaide in August. He set up the Adelaide branch of the society and then moved to Melbourne where he founded a further local office.[40]

The *Blundell* was the second ship and it sailed for Port Adelaide and Melbourne in May 1851 with two hundred and eighteen adults and several children on board. Payments amounted to £1,942, of which £674 had been loaned by the society.[41]

The Great Exhibition was held in London in 1851 and the whole nation was caught up in the excitement it created. A request was made of Prince Albert for the emigrants of the *Blundell* to visit the exhibition on 29 April. The entrance fee for that day should have been £1 each bur the emigrants were given leave 'to view the Crystal Palace before sailing … by an express order from Buckingham Palace, to march in a compact body, under the care of Mrs Chisholm, through and round the Central Avenue'.[42] They were charged 1s. entrance fee each. Samuel Sidney, an assistant commissioner for the exhibition, was a friend and supporter of Caroline, and deputised for her on numerous occasions at emigration meetings. He was probably instrumental in helping to obtain the reduced fee.[43]

The *Athenian*, the society's third ship, left Gravesend on 27 September 1851. It was licensed to sail with 235 emigrants but sailed with 208 souls on board, who paid £1,850 towards the cost of the fare. This amount had been collected in small weekly sums for about eighteen months prior to the voyage. The passengers borrowed £524 from the society, and consisted of forty single females, forty-five single men, and the remainder married men and women with their families. At a meeting on the *Athenian* before she sailed, Lord Shaftesbury commented on the recent news of discovery of gold in the district of Bathurst in Australia. He asked that the emigrants 'be careful, to weigh the matter deliberately, to exercise self-control, and let experience and principle be heard … go out with eyes open, and a determination that by God's blessing nothing should supersede that without which there could be no security or honour for realms, no peace or happiness for families – honest, steady, regular, industrious exertion'. In twelve months 'Mrs Chisholm had been able to collect families of the most industrious and frugal class, numbering one thousand souls, and contributing £5,287', during which period the Government had been 'unable to fill several of their ships with emigrants to whom they gave a free passage, and when filled had only been able to obtain a class whom Earl Grey termed the refuse of workhouses, inferior to convicts'.[44]

The *Athenian* was fitted out with Dr Bowie's invention for better ventilation. As Mackenzie explains, 'this ventilation system comprised two perforated zinc tubes extending from the stem to the stern of the ship, and continued off to the deck. One tube was placed along the roof of the cabin, the other the floor. The first carried off the used air, the latter brought in fresh air. Such was the excellence of Dr Bowie's plan that all the effluvia from the close congregation of so many people and from the large quantity of cooked meat was completely drawn away as it arose.' It brought down the temperature at the equator as well. Dr Bowie also designed a simple contrivance for distilling seawater, which was distributed for sanitary measures.[45] The enhancements meant that the emigrants arrived at their destination in better health than they would have done. The cost of the improvements was more than recouped by the reduction on the medical stores.[46] These systems were incorporated in all the following society ships.

That gentlemen connected with the Australia trade invited Sir Sidney Herbert to a meeting at the London Tavern on 16 January 1852 indicates how well the society was perceived. The discovery of gold and the fear of insufficient labour in the colony had stirred those connected with the trade to act swiftly. Addressed from 14 Old Jewry Chambers, City of London, the letter requesting Sir Sidney to attend the meeting stated that the 'Scheme of Emigration known as the Family Colonisation Loan Society appeared to them to present the readiest means of attaining the object they have in view, and it was determined that efforts should be made to raise a Fund in the City of London with the view of extending the operations of this Society'.[47] The result of the meeting was that a City Committee of the society was set up with offices at 29 Bucklesbury to work in conjunction with Caroline, who still continued to hold meetings at her home in Islington.

The Times must have known of the meeting. In a report printed on the same day, it commented upon the remarkable success of the society, but further noted that the object was now to give it a more commercial bearing to ensure its extension so as to meet the existing emergency, the gold rush. Funds previously employed by the society had been raised by voluntary contributions, but there had been no provision for a proper rate of interest. The report suggested this should now be remedied. Caroline responded in a letter published in *The Times* on 21 January. She explained that, at the time of the formation of the society, the principle of making the scheme self-sustaining by charging a proper rate of premium for interest and risk was not lost sight of, although circumstances prevented its being adopted. She acknowledged that there was now reason for the scheme to be completely recognised and that its wider application, so as to open up a new and sound method for the profitable employment of capital on the part of the public, would soon be realised. Caroline's letter finished with the remark that, 'Gratifying as it may be to have my name mentioned with praise in *The Times*, still I cannot, as the society's parent, allow my promising and healthy child, which I have reared in the suburbs with so much maternal suffering and privation, to be introduced to the world as having the rickets, or suffering from a sickly constitution'.

It was at this time that the Legislative Council of New South Wales voted a sum of £10,000 to be entrusted to the London committee of the society. The report of the executive committee on the best mode of employing the sum placed at its disposal was signed by P. M. Strzelecki, T. S. Atkins, George Hay Donaldson and F. R. Gore. They agreed amongst other things that 'preference shall be given to young married couples with few or no children, or to single persons of both sexes between the ages of 18 and 30; and that males and females shall be sent out as nearly as possible in equal numbers'. The sum was to be applied in 'furtherance of the object of the Family Colonisation Loan Society in such manner as might be arranged between the Secretary of State for the Colonies and the

London Committee of the Society'. The Duke of Newcastle authorised the payment of the money to the society 'without any restrictions as to the mode in which it should be applied'. This was a mark of confidence in the society and its London committee.[48]

The society's fourth ship, the *Mariner*, set sail on 6 March 1852, arriving in Australia in June. There were about 260 emigrants, and they had contributed a greater proportion toward their passage than their predecessors, which meant the society loaned less than £300.[49] The *Francis Walker*, a small ship, sailed with Mrs Chisholm's women on 3 July for Sydney, and arrived at the beginning of October 1852.[50]

The *Scindian*, a ship of nearly 650 tons, departed London with James Cammel as master, carrying 192 adults and seventy-seven children. The ship arrived in Victoria on 16 October 1852. One of the passengers aboard was Peter Lalor (1827–89) who would lead the miners' uprising at Ballarat, Victoria, in 1854, where he would be wounded and his arm amputated. He would later be elected to the Victorian Legislative Assembly (1856–71 and 1874–89) and play a significant part in the politics of the colony.[51]

The *Napaul* sailed shortly after the *Scindian* and arrived in Victoria on 19 October 1852. The ship carried 370 passengers, and Mr T. M. Elgot, writing in *The Cork Southern Reporter* on Thursday 8 July 1852, noted 'nothing could be more complete or better calculated to promote the passengers' comfort'. Mr Elgot was impressed with the 'zinc tube' ventilation and he also commented on Caroline's son, 'a fine young fellow of about nineteen years' who was 'as amiable, assiduous and active as possible in furtherance of his mother's wishes'.[52] Had not Mr Elgot seen it for himself, he 'could not have imagined that such an assemblage could be so docile in accommodating themselves to her wishes'.

The next ship to sail was the *Chalmers* with 256 passengers on board. It arrived in Australia in November 1852.[53]

The *Ballengeich*, in the words of the *Illustrated London News* of 29 August 1852, 'was a fine ship of about 800 tons burden'. It was the 'first vessel that would carry out a number of emigrants on Mrs Chisholm's principles, and under her auspices, who had all, with trifling exceptions, paid their own passage money'. The ship carried about 250 passengers, all in one class; there was no distinction between cabin and steerage passengers.

The *Caroline Chisholm*, a barque of 366 tons, left England in September 1853. There were 144 emigrants on board—twenty-one families, thirteen single women and seventy-eight single men.[54] Among the passengers were twelve young Jewish women who travelled out to Australia under the 'immediate charge of Mrs Chisholm'. These women received help from the Jewish Ladies' Benevolent Loan and Visiting Society.[55]

The total number of emigrants sent out by the society up until 1854, when Caroline returned to Australia, can only be guessed at. The number on board the *Slains Castle*, *Blundell*, *Athenian*, *Napaul*, *Mariner*, *Scindian*, *Chalmers*, *Ballengeich* and *Caroline Chisholm*, of which passenger details are approximately known and given above, number roughly 2,225. Passenger details for the *Francis Walker* are not known, but like the *Caroline Chisholm* it was a small ship. A number of young women sailed with Caroline on the *Ballarat* in 1854. Initially, society members had sailed for Australia on ships that were not charted by the society. In *Memoirs*, Mackenzie suggests that, between September 1850 and July 1852, seven charted or other vessels were despatched, containing 1,288 adults, 475 children and 68 infants, totalling 1,831.[56] An approximation of the numbers sent out by 1854 would be in the region of 2,500 to 3,000.

The ships under the auspices of the London Committee that sailed to Australia after Caroline's departure were the *Bangalore*, *Abdallah*, *Washington Irving*, *Lord Burleigh*, *Nimrod*, *Light of the Age*, *Hanover* and the *Marchioness of Londonderry*. Approximately 710 adults, 282 children and twelve infants travelled to Australia. The passengers contributed roughly £7,790 towards the cost of fares, and the society loaned £6,115.

Repayments to the society after Caroline left for Australia were well below what was expected. Of the 883 emigrants introduced into the colony in 1855, 'only £58.10s. of an outstanding sum of £6,210.12s.6d. had been recovered from the emigrants, whose instant diffusion into the colony made it difficult to collect the funds. The NSW Immigration Agent, H. H. Browne, believed that 'most could have discharged their debt on arrival but chose to evade payment'.[57] A search of the emigrants' files at the Archives Authority of New South Wales suggested that only £247.5s. 0d. had been repaid.[58]

A passenger travelling on one of the ships that sailed in 1855 was a Maybanke Susannah Anderson, née Selfe, also known as Maybanke Wolstenholm. She is known as one of a group 'of forward-thinking, reformist Sydney women, who, along with like-minded men, worked to achieve women's suffrage in New South Wales'. Like Caroline, Maybanke established a girls' school, Maybanke School (later Maybanke College), that went on to gain a 'reputation for its progressive teaching methods and its success in preparing students for Sydney University entrance examinations'. Maybanke was much concerned about the plight of single mothers and their children and wrote a pamphlet in their support, and was later to establish the first free kindergarten at Woolloomooloo in 1895 for working mothers. Maybanke also went on to become Vice-President of the Womanhood Suffrage League of New South Wales.[59]

Caroline insisted that the ships should have improved ventilation methods; a sufficient number of well situated closets, secured to avoid destruction from rough seas; small cabins for privacy; adequate light, and pumps for an ample supply of water; facilities for washing clothes; and, vitally, a supply of food of higher quality than was standard. She would visit Blackwall docks and give directions to carpenters and ship-fitters, inspect the provisions, interview brokers and make arrangements with Government officers.[60] At emigration meetings Caroline encouraged would-be passengers to ensure that whatever ship they sailed on it had these improved facilities. The improvements meant passengers had a better chance of escaping the spread of disease, and certainly could escape the stench of a dormitory. Improvements, of course, meant higher costs and less profit. It is of no surprise that her efforts to upgrade passenger accommodation were seen as unwelcome interference by the shipbuilders, and she was the target of 'vehement and virulent opposition' by ship-owners.[61]

As well as advising would-be passengers to seek out ships with improved facilities, Caroline gave other very practical advice to intending emigrants at her numerous emigration lectures. The *Liverpool Mercury*, for instance, reprinted the verbatim reports of two particular meetings that were held in Liverpool in April 1853. Caroline advised emigrants to line trousers and jackets with blanket pieces to ensure warmth when the ship was passing through cold climates, thereby saving on the necessity to buy an overcoat. She suggested putting clothes in casks rather than trunks. When full of clothes, casks could be rolled even by young children, and after arrival in the colony a cask could be put to numerous uses—on its side as a cradle, as wash tub and so on. She told her audience it was prudent to find a ship that had facilities for washing, saving the poor from 30s to 35s per adult. A ship without washing facilities meant that passengers would have to purchase additional clothing, yet it was a trifling expense for a ship-owner to install a washhouse that added to the comfort and health of those on board. Cleanliness of clothes and body meant a healthy ship. She also told her audience to ensure that the ship had smoothing irons: 'if you get a good iron … you constantly destroy all infection, and consequently it is a very great point to get an ironing stove on board ship'. It was one of the Rules and Regulations to be observed on board the society's vessels that, 'as ventilation and cleanliness are essential to the health and well being of every person on board, it is earnestly recommended, and hoped the Superintendents will strictly enforce, that the Bedding etc from the several Berths be brought on deck twice in each week (viz Tuesdays and Fridays, if practicable) aired and the berths well cleaned'.[62]

Caroline was not requested to give evidence to the select committee appointed to inquire into the working of the Passengers' Act, but she gave evidence to the committee on emigrant ships on 6 April 1854. She again showed no reticence in stating her views very specifically, leaving the committee in no doubt that the 'present space of 18 inches … is not sufficient'. She made 'inquiry of a tailor' who gave her 'a good idea of the measurement' and he told her 'that the average width of the back of a man's coat is 21 inches', and Caroline stated that '12 per cent more space than is given by the last Act is necessary'.[63]

Later in her evidence she was asked about shipwrecks. Anticipating such questioning she had acquired the Admiralty Wreck Chart for 1853 that detailed where ships had been lost. She compared the findings with *Lloyd's Register* to establish that only a small number of 'good ships' had been lost. It is noteworthy that Caroline was the only woman among the twelve witnesses to give evidence to this all-male committee. A further fifteen witnesses gave evidence to the committee in May 1854. None was female.[64] Florence Nightingale, on her return from the Crimean War, chose not to give oral evidence to the Royal Commission on the Health of the Army for political reasons.[65]

One of Caroline's main concerns was that young girls were victimised on board emigrant ships. Charles Dickens was of like mind and published a strongly worded article in *Household Words* in May 1851, condemning the actions of crews of emigrant ships. By a writer using the pseudonym 'Chips', an article on the safety for female emigrants noted:

> One of the greatest and most deplorable hindrances of the emigration of young women to distant colonies, is want of protection. That any class – but more especially women – should ever need protection in British ships manned by British seamen, is a little humiliating; but so many instances of brutality and immorality have been proved, that the treatment of emigrants during their voyage is now occupying the serious attention of the Legislature.[66]

Dickens' concern for the emigration of young women was only one aspect of his philanthropy. He supported thirteen separate hospitals and sanatoriums, and his banking records show he made at least forty-three donations to benevolent and provident funds. He was an officer of various diverse voluntary bodies and campaigned for the education of the poor. He gave various kinds of aid to mechanics' institutes, adult education, soup kitchens, emigration schemes, health and sanitary bodies, model-dwellings associations and recreational societies. He was also a generous supporter of families in distress. After Douglas Jerrold's death in 1857, for instance, Dickens helped raise money for the family.[67]

Dickens was involved with Angela Burdett Coutts (of the banking firm) giving her advice and guidance on a number of her philanthropic projects, but he was particularly involved in the administration of Urania Cottage.[68] The cottage had been set up as a refuge for prostitutes. Other such homes had been set up previously, but in many ways the home that Burdett Coutts and Dickens established was a pioneer. The aim of the cottage in Shepherd's Bush 'was to give the girls back pride in themselves, to train them and then to encourage them to emigrate so that in a new environment they could start a fresh life'.[69] Girls were encouraged rather than punished (although they were expelled for frequent misdemeanours) and the cottage was a home with books and music and a garden, rather than an institution.[70]

On 24 February 1850, Elizabeth Herbert wrote to Caroline informing her she had arranged for Dickens to call on her a few days later at her home in Islington. As a result of the meeting between Caroline and Dickens on 26 February, Dickens published 'A Bundle of Emigrants' Letters' in the inaugural issue of *Household Words*. Dickens wrote to his sub-editor, W. H. Wills, on 6 March 1850, that 'A Bundle of Emigrants' Letters' was a 'little article of my own ... introducing some five or six originals which are extremely good'. The Office Book credits the article to Dickens and Caroline. Caroline supplied the 'original' letters and furnished Dickens with additional information on her experience with emigrants and the society. She probably also supplied him with a copy of her pamphlet the *A.B.C. of Colonisation*, from which Dickens quoted.[71]

A number of articles in *Household Words* were concerned with emigration and the society, but apart from 'Pictures of Life in Australia', which was attributed to Caroline and Richard Henry Horne (Hengist), the other articles were mainly written by Samuel Sidney and Henry Morley.[72] John Sidney, brother of Samuel, contributed 'Milking in Australia' to the first issue.[73] Dickens certainly added support to the cause of emigration, and backed Caroline and her work in both *Household Words* and *Household Narrative*.[74] Martin Chuzzelwit emigrates to America in *Martin Chuzzelwit*, published in 1842, and the Peggottys and the Micawbers emigrate to Australia in *David Copperfield*, published in 1849.

There is speculation as to how Dickens saw Caroline. She is commonly presumed as the model of Mrs Jellyby in *Bleak House*.[75] Mrs Jellyby is a caricature of the woman with a mission: she promotes a scheme for the natives of Borrioboola-Gha on the Niger, and is so absorbed in this work that she neglects her home, her children and her husband, who eventually goes bankrupt. After the failure of the scheme she takes up the rights of women to sit in Parliament, which involves her in even more correspondence than the earlier scheme.

Following his visit to Caroline, Dickens wrote to Angela Burdett Coutts: 'I dream of Mrs Chisholm, and her housekeeping. The dirty faces of her children are my continual companions.'[76] Dickens was amazed at Caroline's incredulity that the girls at Urania Cottage had a piano. He wrote that he regretted he didn't answer: 'Yes—each girl a grand, downstairs—and a cottage in her bedroom—besides a small guitar in the wash-house'.[77] Dickens was disgusted by the way 'certain philanthropists attended to distant causes while ignoring those closer to home'[78] and this is the view he strongly depicts in *Bleak House*. It was not their 'philanthropy' that he objected to. Dickens had more than a passing interest in emigration; he encouraged two of his own sons to emigrate to Australia and his novels and articles deal with the subject.[79] It would not have been Caroline's involvement in emigration that he reacted to, but, based on his brief visit to her home, he believed she was far too concerned in her cause and was neglecting her family.

There are details of Mrs Jellyby's caricature that ring true. In *Bleak House* Dickens describes the 'tarnished brass plate on the door, with the inscription, JELLYBY'. An article in *The Illustrated Magazine of Art* in 1854 describes the Chisholm house as being 'adorned with a very small brass plate, inscribed "Captain Chisholm", which had evidently done years of good service in the East on some bullock trunk or travelling-chest'.[80] Both Dickens and the *Magazine* write of a plump, matronly woman with eyes that look through you.

At the time of Dickens' visit, Caroline was forty-two. Her children were aged fourteen, thirteen, eleven, three, and one year, nine months; Sarah was five or six weeks old (she was to die in August that year). The 1851 Census return for Charlton Crescent, Islington, just over a year later, shows that only Caroline's son Sydney, aged four, and the daughter Caroline, aged two, were at home. Caroline's mother was also present. Archibald was at that time on the high seas travelling back to Australia. Archibald junior was at Oscott College, Birmingham. The exact whereabouts of William and Henry cannot be traced. It was in June 1853 that Florence Nightingale wrote that 'the woman is starving—living upon nine-pence a day'. No record has been found, however, of the Chisholms being bankrupt. We do not know whether the boys were at home when Dickens called. Certainly there was no daughter old enough to do Mrs Chisholm's correspondence, as Miss Caddy Jellyby did for her mother.

Margaret Kiddle, in her biography and an article, firmly took the view that Dickens was an admirer of Caroline, and did not believe that his portrayal of Mrs Jellyby was a caricature based on her. Kiddle refers to another writer who notes that ten years before *Bleak House* was written the African Civilisation Society and Niger Association had been formed, and he felt that their scheme was the model for Mrs Jellyby's.[81] Harriet Martineau[82] and Mrs Arthur Kinnaird[83] have also been suggested as inspiration for Mrs Jellyby.[84] Quite possibly Dickens combined elements of all three women into the caricature.

Kiddle notes Dickens' helpful support of Caroline in *Household Words* but feels 'his description of Mrs Jellyby does not detract from his admiration of Caroline Chisholm and her work'.[85] Kiddle did not have the benefit of knowing the list of contributors and their contributions in the *Household Words* Office Book. We now know who wrote on emigration topics, but she was right in her assumption that Caroline's influence can be seen in the articles. Samuel Sidney, who wrote a number of the articles on emigration, was certainly closely involved with Caroline, but to suggest that Caroline and Dickens were more than just acquaintances, or that Dickens had a high regard for Caroline, is stretching the imagination. There is no information to support Kiddle's viewpoint, and Dickens' letter to Burdett-Coutts would seem to suggest that he had reservations about Caroline as a person. He was known not to have been a friend to Roman Catholics, and this too may have coloured his opinion of Caroline.[86]

Caroline had a closer relationship with Douglas Jerrold. He, a radical Unitarianist, was the son of the actor Douglas William Jerrold, and a friend of Charles Dickens. He was a sailor during the Napoleonic Wars, but left the sea to become a printer, journalist and playwright. As a dramatist he played a prominent role in the development of the English theatre. He was a formidable journalist and humorist. In the 1830s he published frequently in the *Athenaeum*, *Blackwood's Magazine* and *Punch Magazine*. In *Punch* (founded in 1841) Jerrold's articles, many of which were of a social political nature, appeared under the signature 'Q'.[87] Jerrold's publications attacked game laws, war, governmental politics, dishonest lawyers and religious hypocrisy. His plays included *Black-Eyed Susan* (1829), which had a record first-year run of 400 nights in six theatres. His debut at Drury Lane was a domestic melodrama, *The Rent Day* (1832), which contained social criticism. He also wrote short stories, sketches and essays. The *Punch* serial 'Mrs Caudle's Curtain Lectures' (1845) is probably one of his better-known works.

Jerrold was not content to publish material for other magazines; he was editor of the *Illuminated Magazine*, and published *Douglas Jerrold's Shilling Magazine* and *Douglas Jerrold's Weekly Newspaper*. It was in the *Illuminated Magazine* that he supported the 'new People's Charter', and he gave support to Caroline and her society by publishing fifteen articles of hers in his *Weekly Newspaper*.[88]

That Jerrold supported the Chartist cause cannot be doubted. As 'Q' in *Punch* he wrote 'The Milk of Poor Law Kindness', in which he asked when the poor would be 'allowed to belong to this earth [not] as a matter of sufferance, but purely as a matter of right'.[89] In *Punch* on 21 May 1842 he wrote that 'Chartism is born of defeated hope, of disappointment of the fruits of the Reform Act … fostered by … a sordid, remorseless contempt of the inalienable rights of humanity … The Chartists themselves have a degree of intelligence, a power of concentration, a knowledge of the details of public business, heretofore unknown to great popular combinations of dissentients.'[90]

Jerrold did not just write of his support of the cause, but also became actively involved with it. The Peoples' International League was founded in April 1847, the aims of which were to enlighten the British public as to the political condition of foreign countries; to disseminate the principles of national freedom and progress; to advance opinion in favour of the right of every people to self-government and the maintenance of their own nationality; and to promote a good understanding between people of all countries. Jerrold was one of those appointed to be an officer of the council of the League for the following year.[91]

Jerrold is not generally thought to have been a supporter of feminism. Certainly women did not escape his love of satire. However his magazines and his various writings include many feminist articles and references. A contemporary journalist wrote: 'He had considerable faith in woman's capacities for intellectual pursuits, while fully recognising the difficulties under which they laboured when struggling in the battle of life'.[92] His article 'Wrongs of Woman—Hypocrisy of Man' expanded his view that literature in all its forms blinded women to the real nature of their oppression.[93] His *Weekly Newspaper* was a vehicle by which he raised awareness of the issue of female suffrage. He urged his readership to read contemporary works on the subject, and gave book notices of relevant publications.

Jerrold would have appreciated Caroline's endeavours and understood the problems that she had to overcome because of her gender. There is only one known letter between Caroline and Jerrold but that they were well acquainted is not in doubt.[94] There must have been some form of communication between the two as regards the fifteen articles for *Jerrold's Weekly Newspaper*. The *ILN* coverage of Caroline's departure for Australia in 1854 notes that Douglas Jerrold, friend of Caroline Chisholm, was amongst the crowd of well-wishers that gathered to see her off.[95] On hearing that Jerrold wished to be present at her farewell, Caroline wrote that she was pleased to find that he proposed to pay her a farewell visit on board. She went on to add that as he was her first friend connected with the London press it was particularly gratifying to her and she hoped to see him before then.[96] This one letter shows that their relationship was more than just a business matter. It also indicates that Jerrold, rather than Dickens, was Caroline's first introduction to the London press.

Caroline's novelette *Little Joe* leaves us in no doubt of her feelings and admiration of Jerrold:

> they only found three books of devotion, Goldsmith's *Greece, Chambers' Journal* and *Household Words*, with a few copies of the *Herald* and *Empire*, and some numbers of *Lloyd's Weekly Newspaper*... Be careful of *Lloyd's*. ... I was so lucky in getting this number—it gives an account of the death of poor Douglas Jerrold.[97]

> Douglas Jerrold, indeed, was a man ... We hear of testimonials and monuments erected which cost thousands; but fame—fame; what is fame, but the cottager's breath? Thousands upon thousands have felt the generous heroism of Douglas Jerrold's spirit, and if they cannot raise a monument of granite to his memory, they will one of feeling, by leaving his name a cherished one in the hearts of their children.[98]

Interestingly, the extract may give us an indication of Caroline's own choice of reading.

While continuing her work with the society, Caroline undertook lecture tours throughout England, Ireland, France, Germany and Italy, where Pius IX gave her a bust of herself and a papal medal.[99] While in Rome she fetched her son William from the Propaganda College where he had been studying to become a priest. He was unable to continue his studies because of his ill health. Caroline returned to Australia on the *Ballarat,* which sailed from London on 14 April 1854, accompanied by her sons William, Henry and Sydney, and her two daughters, both born in London, Caroline Monica (May 1848) and (Harriet) Monica (July 1851). Caroline had hoped to sail home on the maiden voyage of the auxiliary-screw steamship the *Caroline Chisholm*, commissioned by the society and built in Newcastle-upon-Tyne by W. S. Lindsay. The ship was built to Caroline's specifications for ventilation and space, but was requisitioned for the army to transport soldiers to the Crimea.

At a cost to herself and family, Caroline had achieved much during her time in London. Florence Nightingale, in a letter from Paris to her mother, Fanny, on 2 June 1853 wrote that Caroline badly needed funds: 'Mrs Herbert has just written me word that Mrs Chisholm is living on nine-pence a day having parted with her one maid of all work and not having tasted any meat for weeks'. Florence asked her mother to subscribe £5 on her behalf because 'there is no time to be lost—as the woman is starving'. A testimonial—a subscription—was 'the only way they [Caroline's friends] could think of helping her'.[100] Caroline always insisted that she would not accept money from individuals or religious organisations as she wished to remain, and to be seen to remain, as an independent agent working in the field of emigration. Such knowledge no doubt prompted Florence Nightingale to write in a further letter 'you cannot give her private charity'.[101] The subscription raised between £800 and £900 and was presented to Caroline at a meeting on 9 August 1853 at the London Tavern to mark 'the respect and gratitude of the friends of Mrs Chisholm for her long, arduous, and successful efforts in improving the condition of emigrants to the British Colonies, and especially in promoting the reunion of families, and to present her with a testimonial previous to her departure for Australia'.[102] Mary Hoban notes that other sums were added later.[103]

In one of Caroline's extremely rare personal letters, which follows in full, she confirms she was suffering ill health and details the true extent of the financial problems the family faced. The letter is not dated, but from its content it suggests that it was written at Easter 1852. Archibald left for Australia in March 1851 to act gratuitously as the Colonial Secretary of the society in Melbourne, Australia. Caroline mentions that she will collect Henry from Ireland when she visits in May. Newspaper reports show that she visited Ireland in May 1852. The letter to Bishop Ullathorne reads:

24 Leman Street
Good Friday

Confidential

My Dear Lord

I cannot tell you the comfort, and satisfaction your note has given me for believing it was indirectly your act I felt pained and grieved, indeed so much so that it was with some difficulty I overcame the pain I felt to be able to call upon you the other day—my husband was reconciled to leave his sons, Knowing they were under your care, and had left me particular instructions not to remove them until I left for Australia—withdrawing them was a great trial to me, and involved me in many difficulties at a time I was in a helpless state of health and had heavy cares regarding my work. His Eminence who knew I had been ordered to remove even my infant on account of my health when he heard of my having the boys at home offered to pay the difference between what I could afford, and the charges of Se[d]gley,[104] but I could not bring myself to accept of this offer, and have therefore parted earlier than I ought with Dear William by accepting of Cardinal Fransoni's offer;[105] and sent dear Henry to Ireland—the poor child is wretched and when I go there in May I shall take him home with me.[106] Archy is a great comfort to me, but his education has been checked and the following out of my vocation will I fear be a lasting disadvantage to them—and yet my Lord I dare not give up my work it hangs about me as a duty, and will not permit me to consider perhaps so much as I ought the sacrifices I am bringing upon others through their love, and obedience to me—as I am now as I write relieving a burthened and oppressed spirit I will tell your Lordship the real object and aim of my life, I did not marry until I had told Captain Chisholm to what my whole mind was devoted—it is now twenty five years since after much thought I had a fixed impression on my mind that Crime would be made self supporting. I consulted a friend one of age, and experience who knew my mind, he reasoned, and told me that to carry out my views I must have more of public support, and confidence than I could ever expect to gain, that wealth, that influence, were needed, and amongst the improbabilities in my way he named the necessity of a voyage to New South Wales, the dread of misusing my object kept me long from embracing the Faith I now enjoy—seeking nothing, but waiting, watching and working I have gained some influence, and if my health is spared me the coming importance of the treatment of prisoners will give me as fair a chance of a trial as any one else. This object is the real reason of my refusing the govt funding, what I think probable is that my claim on public confidence will be greater by doing so—

I have thought it prudent not to speak of my plan or intention—but to continue working where I am doing much good until the finger of providence points the way—I often wonder why I am selected for so much good many would receive with joy, a burthen I am often too unwilling to bear.

Entreating your prayers and blessing
I remain
Sincerely Yours
Caroline Chisholm[107]

This is a most poignant letter and tells us a great deal of Caroline's character, her circumstances and her conscience. You can almost feel the emotion seeping through her words. She is obviously very concerned that she was unable to carry out Archibald's 'particular instructions' not to remove their sons from Sedgley Park School, yet financial difficulties impelled her to do so. Even though Archibald was concerned that the boys should remain at Sedgley, Caroline did not feel able to accept financial help to pay the school fees. Paying school fees for three boys must have hit the small family budget considerably. Boys were admitted to the school between the ages of seven and fourteen. The fees were fifteen guineas per year, with an entrance fee of one guinea. There was an extra half guinea charge for a boy to learn Latin, and additional charges for French, drawing and dancing, as masters would have to be brought in to teach these subjects. The Park provided clothing, but boys had to bring their own wigs. Clothing had to be durable rather than fancy, probably made from corduroy, and would include a short jacket with waistcoat and knee breaches. If parents themselves wanted to supply the clothes, the fee was reduced to twelve guineas.[108] Even if Caroline and Archibald paid the reduced fee and the boys did not have additional coaching, they would still have had to find thirty-six guineas a year, a large sum.

The first group meeting of the Family Colonisation Loan Society was held at Charlton Crescent on 14 April 1850, and from then on Caroline's diary was filled with meetings up and down the country (see Appendix 4). It is no surprise that Caroline wrote in the above letter that she had 'heavy cares regarding my work'. The sadness that Caroline and Archibald must have felt at the death of their child, the tremendous stress of trying to cope with their financial burdens and the continual very busy work schedule undoubtedly must have had an effect upon Caroline's health. As Florence Nightingale commented, in the battle to make ends meet food may well have taken a lower priority. At the time of Archibald's departure to Australia in March 1851, Caroline was five months' pregnant with another daughter, Harriet Monica, who was born on 24 July 1851. Another pregnancy could well have taken a further toll on her health, and she had to cope with all the problems on her own.

The letter gives us an insight into Caroline's concern for her children. She is obviously anxious at having to send William to Rome earlier than she had anticipated, and upset to know that Henry is 'wretched' in Ireland. She is aware that one of the implications of her following her 'vocation' is that it will be a 'lasting disadvantage' to her children. Yet at the same time she feels she cannot give up her work that 'hangs about me as a duty'. The letter leaves the reader with no doubt of the inner turmoil Caroline felt trying to balance her work with the lives of her children, and an appreciation of why she had an 'oppressed spirit'. This is something that women today, in trying to balance a career with family commitments, understand only too well.

It would seem that Caroline had long cherished the idea of working, like Elizabeth Fry, to help prisoners. The advice of a friend had obviously suggested that she must go to New South Wales. Caroline would have been about nineteen at the time, three years before she married Archibald Chisholm. There is a tantalising newspaper cutting found in the scrapbooks purchased by Mary Hoban that were originally in the possession of Caroline's grandson, and are now held at the Immigration Museum in Melbourne. A small scrap of newspaper, without date or title of paper, mentions a banquet given by Mr Wyndham Harding on board the *Ballengeich* before it sailed, and at which a toast was proposed to Mrs Chisholm. Mrs Chisholm replied to the toast:

> I rise as a wife and mother to acknowledge the toast my friend Mr Harding has given. And I will take this opportunity of mentioning one or two facts in my life which may be interesting as showing how I was led to the task in which the greater part of that life has passed. The idea of life being a task leading, when well performed, on to the inexpressible happiness of heaven, I learnt on the knee of Legh Richmond when a mere …

The newspaper article has not been found, and there appears to be no connection between Legh Richmond (1772–1827) and Caroline. Richmond was inducted into the Rectory at Turvey in July 1805 and he took up his duties in October. Although Turvey is in Bedfordshire, it is close to the Northamptonshire border between Olney and Bedford. Many residents in neighbouring towns and villages attended Richmond's church in Turvey, for it was rare for a clergyman of ability to have evangelical views. He published the *Annals of the Poor*, which included the stories 'The Dairyman's Daughter', 'The Young Cottager' and 'The Negro Servant'. The Religious Tract Society reprinted these stories in 1814. Without evidence one can only guess that Caroline's suggestion that she 'learnt on the knee of Legh Richmond' refers to her reading his religious tracts. It would be speculative to suggest that he was the friend who suggested she should go to New South Wales. However, he held two full services at Turvey on Sundays and a lecture for the young in the evening. On Tuesday nights he gave lectures, held in cottages of the poor. He also established a Sunday school that he attended regularly. It is known that he held meetings at Kettering in Northamptonshire, and preached at All Saints Church in Northampton, the adjoining parish to the Church of the Holy Sepulchre that Caroline and her family attended.

While Caroline faced problems at home, Archibald was working hard on behalf of the society in Australia. He too had problems. Before Archibald left England the society set up, with the help of Coutts and Company, the facility that enabled its colonial agents to forward repayments of loans to London through the Bank of Australasia's branches in Adelaide, Hobart, Melbourne and Sydney. It also enabled the agents to forward remittances received from settlers, small amounts collected on a weekly or monthly basis, to assist their relatives in Britain or to help them with the cost of the fare to Australia. Archibald arrived in Adelaide in August 1851 and shortly afterwards established an office of the South Australian committee of the society in King William Street. Amongst the members of the committee were leaders of several different churches. Archibald encouraged 'the labouring colonists' to take advantage of the banking arrangement, and collected £3,000 in gold.[109] He noted that twenty-eight parents, thirty-eight brothers and sisters, thirteen children and three wives had received money through the banking scheme to help them emigrate to Australia.[110]

The society's emigrants on the *Slains Castle* and the *Blundell* were slow to repay their loans. Legal advice was sought on the possibility of obtaining repayment through legal proceedings, but Archibald was advised that agreements made in England could not be enforced in Australia. It does not appear that any legal action was taken, but Archibald wrote a long letter to the *Adelaide Observer* on 9 August 1851 appealing to those who had not repaid their loans to do so. Archibald also set up an enquiry register in conjunction with the London office of the society, whereby relatives at home could trace relatives in Australia. Archibald received one hundred and forty three enquiries of settlers on behalf of their relatives in England.[111]

At the end of October 1851 Archibald appointed William C. Atchison to take his place as colonial agent in Adelaide and moved to Melbourne where he set up an office at 110 Swanston Street. It was not the best time to be setting up an office. Melbourne was flooded with diggers from overseas all trying to equip themselves and move on to the goldfields, and able-bodied men deserted the town for the gold digging areas. The cost of food rapidly increased. It is little wonder that Archibald and the Melbourne committee of the society had great difficulty in securing repayment of the society's loans. As Archibald had done in Adelaide, he considered but did not pursue legal proceedings.[112] On 14 May 1852, however, *The Argus* reported that the committee had collected nearly £4,000 from local donations, which was remitted to London to enable 474 people to emigrate to Victoria.

The emigrants on the *Slains Castle*, *Blundell* and *Athenian* arrived in Melbourne at a time when accommodation was difficult to find. Melbourne was rapidly becoming the immigrant-clearing house for the goldfields.[113] This necessitated the committee meeting every month, with additional special meetings. Governor La Trobe offered to accommodate some of the emigrants in the Immigration Depot.[114] Archibald Chisholm and the local society proposed the establishment of its own Emigrants' Home, requesting a plot of land and a grant of £500. La Trobe and the Legislative Council accepted the proposal, making a few alterations and stipulations. The committee returned £40 to the council, having only spent £460 on a wooden one-room structure, sixty by twenty feet, that could house about sixty women and children. Caroline sent out eighteen tents to house the men and boys. Archibald continued his work with the added duties of supervisor of the home. The immigrants were expected to pay a small accommodation fee, but Archibald had little time to collect the money, draw up and enforce rules and regulations or record the numbers passing through the home. Immigration Reports however indicate that immigrants from four ships stayed at the home between October 1852 and early March 1853. Thereafter the inflow of immigrants dropped and other shelters were able to accommodate society immigrants, and the home and the plot were returned to the Government.[115]

Quite possibly the volume of work and the difficulties that Archibald faced can account in part for the diary entry of Thomas Lyle who sailed on the *Nepaul* that arrived in Melbourne in 1852. Thomas wrote of the bushrangers who continually dragged the tent-dwellers out of their abode and then robbed them of what little they had. He went on to say: 'it became the usual thing for those who had tents to stop up half of the night with loaded guns keeping watch and continually firing them off all night; when another set would take your place and do the same and it was really alarming to hear guns going off almost every minute with the expectation of a chance shot about your head'. Thomas 'left the tents in disgust' and went on to Collingwood about two miles from the town.[116]

During the period of organisation for the reception depot, two members of the Melbourne committee, in rotation, were visiting all ships that arrived with immigrants in Port Phillip. The remittance system, open to all settlers and not just the society's members, was working well. In July 1852 Archibald asked that his resignation from the committee be accepted in order that he may proceed to New South Wales to establish a branch there, and to organise the appointment of a colonial agent in Brisbane. The financial boost to the society's funds in London meant that it could now pay their colonial agents. Archibald, then fifty-four, felt that there was no longer an urgent need for Caroline and for him to continue their heavy labours. The separation from his wife had put an additional financial burden on them, and in 'justice to our children', it would be better if an agent be appointed who had more leisure and means than he and his wife had at their disposal. However, with so few men in Melbourne it proved difficult to find a suitable replacement for Archibald, and he continued to act as colonial agent. There is no evidence that Archibald travelled to Sydney or Brisbane. A branch was set up in Sydney, but organised from London.[117]

Archibald gave evidence before the Legislative Council Select Committee on the Present System of Immigration, the report of which was published in January 1853. He felt that the distance from Britain and lack of knowledge of Australia worked against emigration to the colonies: he believed that if more information on Australia were distributed abroad a higher number of emigrants would choose Australia as their destination. When requested to give evidence before the Committee on a second occasion, he asked if he could do so in writing.

It is not often remarked upon, but Archibald's support of Caroline and her work was invaluable. He physically, emotionally and financially supported his wife to the best of his abilities as his work in Adelaide and Melbourne clearly demonstrates. His efforts too deserve wider recognition.

It is an indication of the appreciation of Caroline's work that a portrait of her was hung at the Royal Academy in 1852. This painting shows Caroline

Chisholm sitting at a desk, holding papers, with the map of Australia in the top left-hand corner. The original now resides at the State Library of New South Wales. Measuring 99.8 x 124.5 cm, it precisely matches the 1852 lithography by Thomasophin Fairland and is clearly inscribed on the bottom left 'painted by A C Hayter'. The State Library purchased the painting from the Godolphin Gallery in Dublin in September 1983.

There has been considerable confusion in the past as to who painted the portrait. Margaret Kiddle wrote that an obscure painter, Angelo Collen Hayter, executed the painting that gave a very good likeness of her.[118] Mary Hoban, however, attributes the painting to the 'Queen's portrait painter, Sir George Hayter' who had 'previously made a drawing of her [Caroline] the reproduction of which he was not very pleased, although Caroline had written to thank him for the compliment to herself and the "cause of Colonization"'.[119]

The confusion very likely arose from the fact that Caroline wrote from her home at 3 Charlton Crescent, Islington, London on 11 April 1850 to Sir George Hayter. In that letter she thanked Sir George for his 'kindness in taking my likeness'. An annotation dated 8 June 1854 reads: 'This note alludes to a drawing which I made of Mrs Chisholm to be engraved for the *Illustrated News* which was done but very badly from the drawing alluded to by her in the above. George Hayter'.[120] There is no doubt that Queen Victoria's portrait artist did indeed do a likeness of Caroline Chisholm. On reading the miscellaneous papers relating to Caroline Chisholm held by the State Library of New South Wales, it becomes clear that Caroline's two daughters, Caroline and Monica (Harriet), also believed that Sir George Hayter did the painting of their mother with the map.[121] No doubt such evidence convinced Mary Hoban that the artist was Sir George. Sir George

Hayter, however, definitely did not portray Caroline with the map in the background. Angelo Collen Hayter executed this painting.

In all likelihood the picture for which Caroline thanked Sir George Hayter is that which appears in the *Illustrated Magazine of Art.*[122] This is a wood engraving by an unknown engraver and is badly done. Studies of Sir George Hayter's archives have not thrown any further light on the matter. That both Sir George Hayter and Angelo Collen Hayter felt inspired to do a portrait of Caroline Chisholm shows the tremendous appreciation of her and her work.

Caroline ceased any active part in the society when she left England for Australia in 1854, but from the time of her return to Britain in 1846 until her departure, her work and achievements in the field of emigration were considerable. She carried out her promise to settled emigrants when collecting their statements prior to leaving Australia in 1846. Emancipists' wives and families had been sent out free of charge, and the children who had been left behind in Britain were reunited with their parents. Caroline founded the Family Colonisation Loan Society, and by insisting on better on-board provisions and giving evidence to the various parliamentary committees, she helped improve the Passenger Acts, benefiting all who emigrated. As the name of the society suggests, its aim was to send complete families out to Australia, many of whom were skilled tradespeople from the lower middle class. The numbers which the society sent out under Caroline's leadership and that of the London Committee after her departure to Australia, approximately 5,000, may seem like a drop in the ocean when compared with the vast numbers who emigrated under the various government schemes (nearly 1.5 million between 1821 and 1900),[123] but the emigrants that the society sent 'raised the moral standard of colonial society, and their own moral well-being was increased by their freedom from want in the new land'.[124] The society was in operation at a time when emigration was on the increase because of the potato famine in Ireland and the discovery of gold in Australia. Caroline's respect and commitment to the greater comfort and the health of the emigrants influenced the way emigrants in general were treated. She set the standard that others in the field followed. She had hoped to improve moral standards by encouraging her emigrants to pay for their own passage to Australia, but the society failed to recover many of the loans it made.

Caroline supported the Colonial and International Postage Association, which advocated that there should be a reduction of colonial postage rates, and through her efforts a system of post-office orders between Britain and the colonies was established.[125] With the assistance of Coutts and Company and with Archibald's help as colonial agent, she was able to establish a scheme for settled emigrants to send money home to Britain to assist family members to emigrate. A system was also put in place whereby family members in Britain could trace and communicate with their loved ones in Australia.

As Samuel Smiles noted in *Self-Help*, Caroline was someone who acted upon philanthropic deeds, rather than just lecturing on the subject and letting others take the strain. (See pages 161/162)

Victorian Gold Digging

AUSTRALIA REVISITED 1854–1866 & AGAIN IN BRITAIN 1866–1877

Throughout 1852 and 1853 the *Illustrated London News* carried numerous articles on gold digging in Australia and California. The presence of gold in Australia was known nearly twenty years earlier but the colonial government had played down the fact. They feared 'the discovery, for the excitement of a gold rush might make the large convict and ex-convict element in NSW uncontrollable'.[1] The government was proved correct. When the new gold find became known in May 1851 Bathurst was drained of its labourers, squatters were deserted by their shepherds, and smiths were extremely busy making pickaxes.[2] Sydney soon began to feel the effects of an exodus from the town. Melbourne's population was depleted as diggers left for Bathurst at a time when the colony of Victoria had only just won its independence from New South Wales. To counter the outflow, Melbourne citizens offered a reward 'for the discovery of a profitable gold-field within 200 miles of the city'.[3] In August 1851 gold was found 'on the banks of a stream at Ballarat, some fifty miles north-westward of Geelong'.[4] By October, Melbourne and Geelong were almost emptied of many classes of the male population.[5]

With the discovery of gold there was no longer a need to encourage emigration. As Kiddle remarks, 'the gold discoveries had brought such a flood of new people into the colony, and … hastened the pace of what had been a leisurely pastoral society … The colonies were filled with a lusty, thrusting development, quickened by the results of the discovery of gold.'[6]

The rapidly growing colonisation in Australia meant that Caroline began to slip from view. She returned to Australia on the aptly named *Ballarat*, arriving in Melbourne on 12 July 1854. Writing to Angela Burdett Coutts to thank her for inviting her to dinner before she left England, Caroline told her of the rise in the cost of fares due to the demand for ships to take soldiers to the Crimean War. The outlay for her journey with the family was £100 for Caroline, for half a cabin seven feet by seven; £40 each for the boys in second-class accommodation, but taking their meals with Caroline; and £21 each for the young girls, with the addition of a family contract of £25.[7] The subscription that was raised by Caroline's friends, and to which Florence Nightingale contributed, must have been very welcome indeed.

The *Ballarat* was late in docking in Melbourne and many people from amongst the large crowd that had assembled to meet Caroline and her family had dispersed by the time they disembarked. A welcome meeting was therefore arranged to be held at the Mechanics Institute on 31 August. It was a great success. A second meeting, organised by the committee of the *FCLS*, was held towards the end of September, to welcome Caroline back to Australia and also to thank Captain Chisholm for all his efforts in Victoria. Without any financial reward, Archibald had worked tirelessly in setting up the two local branches of the *FCLS*, running the remittance schemes, setting up and running a reception depot and meeting emigrant ships. His commitment demonstrates his dedication and devotion to his wife's cause. In recognition of Caroline's philanthropy, and Archibald's gratuitous work as colonial agent, the committee proposed that a testimonial be raised. After some wrangling, the Legislative Council agreed to allocate the sum of £5,000, provided half the amount was raised by public subscription. Because of difficulties within the province, Caroline did not receive the cheque until 1855. In the meantime the Chisholms were in such financial difficulties that the testimonial committee had 'to advance the family "a small sum of money" to put them in a position of earning their livelihood'. The money was allocated to the purchase of a large store for the family.[8]

Prior to Caroline's arrival in Melbourne, Archibald had tried to find ways of enhancing the family's finances. Mary Hoban notes that Messrs Chisholm & Son had a small warehouse off Flinders Lane East, but it did not make a fortune.[9] There was also a small store in A'Beckett Street.[10] On 28 November 1854 Archibald reached retirement age. He had served the necessary number of years in India and was therefore entitled to a major's pension, and allowed to use the title as a courtesy. The retirement pension and the testimonial allowed the family to purchase a retail store in Elizabeth Street. The store was well sited and it was hoped that it would capture its fair share of the goldfields trade,[11] but it was not a good time to open a store. There had been many cases of insolvency towards the end of 1854 and prices and wages were falling. The Chisholms suffered as others suffered.

During the first few months of 1855 additional monies from the testimonial allowed the family to purchase the Rogers and Harpers general store at Kyneton. One of the Melbourne stores was turned into a depot.

Archibald ran the store with the help of the older boys, Archibald junior, nineteen, William, eighteen, and Henry John, sixteen. The store that later became known as Chisholm Brothers, East Kyneton, and those at 12 A'Becket Street and 268 Elizabeth Street, Melbourne, sold wines, spirits, provisions, drapery and ironmongery.[12]

Archibald attended the local magistrate's court as a justice of the peace. The younger members of the family took lessons with their governess, Mrs Anne Clinton, who lived on the premises. Caroline stayed in Melbourne at the premises at A'Beckett Street, continuing to help the emigrants find employment and organising shelter sheds. She remained there for three years, travelling to and from Kyneton.[13]

In mid-1856 Major Chisholm was 'invited to present as a candidate for the new parliament for Kyneton Boroughs, which included Woodend and Malmsbury'.[14] He felt unable to accept the offer; his nominees then asked Archibald junior to stand in his place, and he accepted the nomination. Caroline supported her son on a number of occasions, but her support worked for and against young Archibald, as did the religion of the family. One of his opponents suggested, 'Mr Chisholm's pretensions were based *solely* on the public services of his mother'. Young Archibald was a year short of the age of majority (twenty-one), the minimum requirement for candidature, and it was debatable that he met the property requirement.[15] Archibald lost the election by 126 votes. He did not stand again.

It would have been important for Caroline to find employment that befitted her status as a well-known and popular woman. As Roberts notes, 'for many working-class families working in a shop carried more social status than working either in a factory or in domestic service'.[16] There would have been few other opportunities open to her.

In the novelette *Little Joe*,[17] Caroline reflects on the 'ugly' willow pattern that her characters are compelled to buy, and obviously sees the disadvantage of selling crockery in sets. She wrote: 'it would be a great advantage for a young wife to be able to purchase her one dish and six plates of an elegant pattern, that she could add to as her circumstances improved or her family increased'.[18] She also comments on pickle jars and 'the difficulty of getting the pickles out of the bottle', which could spoil a good dinner. 'The bottles ought to be large enough to admit into them a good-sized spoon.'[19] Caroline's ever-practical nature shines through.

Not everybody welcomed Caroline back to Melbourne. William Howitt was extremely critical of her in a letter he wrote from Bendigo on 23 April 1854. He firmly believed that the statements Caroline had made at meetings in the manufacturing districts of England to encourage people to emigrate to Victoria were 'totally untrue'.[20] In Britain Caroline had indeed been unaware of the squatters' monopoly in Victoria. Howitt had himself experienced the hardships prospectors faced when travelling to the diggings, and the appalling living conditions that confronted them when they arrived. His censure of Caroline arose because he believed she had no knowledge or experience of life in Victoria, or of the gold-digging routes and living conditions in the gold-prospecting areas. Writing a postscript to his letter on 1 March 1855, he said that he was not disappointed to learn that Mrs Chisholm had 'candidly at a public meeting in Melbourne declared her discoveries of the painful reality that awaited her'.[21]

No doubt spurred on by Howitt's comments, Caroline had set out within three months of her arrival to discover for herself the conditions in the gold digging areas. She experienced the problems of getting through the thick mud of the Black Forest, was shocked by the large array of public houses, and felt that the 'great grievance is that they [the men] cannot get the land'.[22] The conditions she saw resulted in her campaigning even more strongly for the 'unlocking of the land' for the small farmer. She wrote a number of letters to *The Argus*. One in particular, written on 9 December 1854, shortly after the Eureka Stockade,[23] deplored the incident which had 'stained the hands of the people with blood' and hit out at the squatters' monopoly and the Wakefield system.[24] Caroline continued her campaign until her health broke down towards the end of 1857. She was beginning to suffer from the kidney disease that blighted the rest of her life.

Caroline raised her idea of shelter sheds (later to become known as 'Chisholm Shakedowns') with the newly appointed Governor Hotham. She had seen for herself that the high cost of accommodation and food at the numerous inns along the track often made them impractical for travellers. A result of this was that men often travelled to the goldfields alone. Caroline suggested that the sheds should be paid for out of the Immigration Tax Fund. Despite strong opposition from the Legislative Council, Governor Hotham approved the scheme. On Friday, 27 July 1855 the Supplement to the *Government Gazette* requested tenders by noon on Friday 10 August for the erection of Shelter Sheds or Protection Posts to be built at Essendon, Keilor, Robertson's, The Gap, Gisborne, The Black Forest, Woodend, Carlsruhe, Malmesbury and Elphinstone. The sheds were to be constructed of 'hardwood timber and the walls and roof to be covered with hardwood palings, the floors to be laid with joists and proper boards and all doors and windows to be fixed where indicated or necessary'. There was to be 'one large boiler and two fireplaces to be fixed in cookhouses, with sleeping berths to be fitted up and properly divided by partitions'.[25] The sheds were to be an easy day's walk apart, and they were to provide accommodation for single men, single women, and families in separate living quarters. For those travellers who provided their own beds the charges for the shelter sheds were 6d. and 3d. for adults and children respectively. Furnished beds were 1s. for adults, 6d. for children. Beds in a small room were 1s. 6d. For cooking with wood and water the charges were 6d. per adult and 3d. per child.[26] Such charges enabled families to travel together to the gold digging areas. Caroline helped manage the shelter sheds, travelling the length of the route on a great number of occasions. The sheds were a great success. Others had been planned, but, either due to financial difficulties or to Caroline's ill health, no more were built. Interestingly, Eneas Mackenzie, Caroline's first biographer, was acting honorary secretary to the Shelter Sheds Committee.[27] Eneas Mackenzie returned to Australia between 1855 and 1861.[28]

Caroline did not leave Melbourne and settle permanently in Kyneton until 4 December 1857. Her friends in Melbourne gave her a farewell party with 'tea and dessert' at the Duke of Kent Hotel in Lonsdale Street. Dr Early, the medical superintendent of the Immigrants' Home, gave the farewell speech. He conveyed best wishes for health and happiness to Caroline and her family. Her friends and neighbours regretted her going, for they had appreciated her 'untiring energy for the good of the neighbourhood, and our respect for your many private virtues and public services, which have endeared you, not only to us individuals, but also to a large portion of the colonists of Victoria'. Dr Early went on to say that, 'in you we have always found a friend to console us in times of distress, a good adviser in times of prosperity'.[29] In her reply Caroline commented that 'people had wondered why she had not been exerting herself lately to the cause of emigration, but the reason of her apparent supineness was that she declined to have anything to do with sending single men to the diggings and single women onto the streets. What she wanted to see in force was a scheme of family colonization.'[30]

Caroline's health problems persisted. In 1859 on the advice of her doctors the family moved from Kyneton to Sydney for the better climate as the 'only chance of her recovery'.[31] As she improved she conducted political lectures on various subjects including the secret ballot, free selection before the surveying of new settlements, early closing of shops and the poor conditions of city housing. The first was held in front of a 'far from numerous' audience at the Prince of Wales Theatre in Sydney on Friday, 8 July 1859, and Caroline took as her theme 'The Progress of Public Opinion on the Land Question, Election, Ballot, and Manhood Suffrage; State-aid, Payment of Members, the Land League'.[32] The audience may have been on the small side, but among those present were The Hon. Charles Cowper, the Hon. J. Robertson,[33] Dr Bland, M.L.C., and a few other members of both houses of the legislature. That they saw fit to attend Caroline's lecture shows in no small measure the esteem in which they held her and is indicative of her influence in the community.

Caroline began by commenting upon the general belief that 'no woman ought to have any opinions whatever as regards politics'. She 'had seen a good deal of life and had herself seen good cause to adopt certain well-defined political opinions; and she would fearlessly remark that the political evils of which they had heard so much complaint, resulted from the blunders of their political leaders'. Later in the lecture she intimated that there had been 'serious objections … urged against a lady appearing before the public, but she would state her reasons for taking that course. If a man had property, and was going to die, he might leave it to whomsoever he liked, but his ideas or his experience must die with him. Now she did not want her experience to die with her, but if she had one good thought she wished to impart it; she wanted the mind to wear out with the body.'

The main thrust of Caroline's lecture was the new Electoral Act, 'which acted as a sledge hammer in its application to all existing abuses'. Caroline asked the audience 'why should a property vote instead of an individual? ... A property ought not to be consulted in parliamentary representation, which should be based on individuals alone.' Caroline then proceeded to speak of the ballot, of which she highly approved, even saying 'it was worth coming sixteen thousand miles to get hold of it', and that emigrants should write home and tell their friends and families what a 'boon the ballot was'. Caroline wanted the advances in political reform in New South Wales to encourage reforms at home in Britain. She urged her audience not to rely on petitions to the legislature to achieve universal suffrage, 'for petitions were packed up and never read', but to use 'the only legitimate means of influence ... small private meetings and the Press'.

The land question was also raised—'that instinctive longing to possess a piece of land upon which a man might set his foot as owner, and on which he might make a home'. The land system in the colony needed improvement as it was impossible for 'men to get farms'. For this reason, she stated, she no longer advised female immigration. What was required was a new land system, for the old one could no longer be patched. She assured her audience that 'the most respectable females were looking towards the colony, but their hindrance was the difficulty at present in getting a home'.

Caroline spoke of the importance of reading newspapers and alluded to her personal circumstances and the suggestion that she should open a school. Her sense of humour, in spite of her ill health, had not escaped her. She suggested that she had 'always thought a school for legislators would be a very useful institution, and the idea seemed to have been carried out, for she had nine of such pupils before her' at the lecture.

She must also have noticed the two bank directors who were in her audience, for she expounded upon the necessity of a Post Office order system that would thereby save the sixpence discount which she 'had often had to pay'. She believed the 'sin of great cities' to be the lack of facilities for working men to send money to their wives and families.

The second lecture was held on Monday, 20 December 1860, in the middle of the elections, on the subject of 'Free Selection before Survey', at the Temperance Hall in Sydney.[34] For many years Caroline had keenly supported the campaign for free selection which 'advocated the right of settlers to select land even before the under-resourced Lands Department had surveyed it'.[35] On this occasion there was a very large audience and the heat and the inability to hear Caroline at the back of the room caused problems. At the commencement of the meeting Caroline asked that the ladies present be seated on the platform. The *Empire* reported on her 'graceful but firm attack on the old prejudice which resents any public attempt of woman to meddle with politics'.

The land question had interested Caroline for many years. She showed the meeting a number of documents that proved she had not only thought deeply about the subject, but had also done something to promote it. In no uncertain terms she attacked the squatters and criticised the unrepresentative upper house, which she referred to as 'The Club'. Caroline wanted land for the unemployed, but freehold land, not 'mere leasehold or occupancy'. She praised Dr John Dunmore Lang, in spite of the difficulties he had thrown in her way in the past, as 'the only man who was working to obtain [land] for the use and the support of the people'. She drew attention to what she called the 'squatters' dodge', or the double standards of the squatters: they demanded that the land should be surveyed before settlement by small farmers and working-class people, knowing only too well that such an undertaking would take years to complete. Yet those same squatters had obtained their vast lands, in most cases illegally, before a surveyor had looked at them.

Caroline felt free selection would increase the gold price. The miners did not want to risk all their capital at the diggings, but if they were allowed small farms, and had their wives and families with them, they would then invest their capital, which would bring benefits to all.

She was not afraid to raise the Chinese issue—the disagreeable attitudes of Europeans towards Asians and the political debate on restricting Chinese immigration. She warned her audience that if she was given the opportunity to vote in the House of Representatives she would not use her vote against the Chinese.

Her lecture closed with mention of the payment of parliamentarians. Paying members, Caroline believed, would allow parliament to be open to all classes, not just those who had money and time, and the privileges that went with them. But she 'urged her hearers to act cautiously and with dignity during the present crisis, so that their worst enemies would be forced to respect them'.

Lecture three, on the 'The Early Closing Movement',[36] was held at St Benedict's Young Men's Society in Sydney on Monday, 18 February 1861. In Sydney the shops were open until ten o'clock at night. Again there was a large audience and a large number of women amongst them. Caroline had become 'a focus for women breaking tradition and involving themselves in debates on public affairs'.[37] Mr A. Chisholm (Archibald junior), the president of the society, was on the platform with other dignitaries. On this occasion Reverend Father Cornish, the pastor of the district, occupied the chair. The Early Closing Movement was a subject that Lord Shaftesbury had firmly supported in England.

Caroline commenced by referring to speakers at a meeting held at the Temperance Hall. The orators had 'condemned the ladies as being the sole causes of late shopping'. Caroline admitted that the ladies did shop late, 'but she was quite certain that it was the primary fault of the gentlemen. Why did not the legislators of Macquarie Street set an example by closing early?' The gentlemen, instead of helping out at their homes, left early for work and stayed out late. 'Consequently the women had to defer shopping till the evening.' Caroline was concerned for the women who worked in the shops, having to face 'insults and temptations ... when going to their homes at that late hour'. She also dwelt on 'the conduct of husbands to their wives, domestic life in Sydney and on the desirability of having husbands returning home early and of remaining there'. Caroline advised the ladies present at the lecture to read the newspapers.

Caroline took the opportunity to question the belief that 'the squatters were the pioneers of civilisation in the colony, and of the settlement of the interior'. She spoke at some length on the part she had taken in bringing people to the colony and of getting them settled in the interior, and maintained that she was as much a pioneer of settlement of the interior as any person in the colony.

The last lecture, 'Our Home Life', was given on 13 June 1861 at the Temperance Hall in aid of the Free Reading Room established by the NSW Alliance for the Suppression of Intemperance. Over six hundred people attended.[38] Mr W. Bland was placed in the chair. Caroline began by speaking in support of the Free Reading Room: she trusted that would receive all due backing so that it might continue to exercise its beneficial influence upon the less opulent classes. She went on to ask 'What was a home?'. The prevalent idea appeared to be that of a small cottage and garden. This led her to discuss the Land Bill that would become either a 'great reality' or a 'great sham'. She had confidence in the governor and the then present ministry, but they were too much disposed to wait for other people to do their work for them. Caroline felt she was paying too high a rent for very small rooms that would not allow her to walk about in her crinolines (which she felt were monstrous things). She talked about bad roads, and called attention to the Sydney Government Domain, which was a dangerous place for mothers and children after seven at night. At that time, Sydney was experiencing great difficulties with vast numbers of homeless children and juvenile prostitution.[39]

Caroline referred the listeners to the report of the state of the working classes drawn up by Mr Parkes and questioned why the land surrounding the diggings was to be left unpopulated. She believed great evil resulted from the families of gold miners being left in Sydney. She was appalled that as many as seventy human beings might be herded together in a house of six rooms. She cited other such cases, and all due to low wages and the necessity of letting out rooms to pay the butcher and the baker. Caroline believed hundreds of men had gone to their grave because they had no homes. What also appalled her was that many men who had come to find gold, and had done so, had left the colony as soon as they could purely because they could not get a home. Caroline mentioned the fine mansions of bachelors and the exclusivity of male clubs, especially the Australian Club in Bent Street, and the detrimental effect they had on the home.

She then moved on to speak of the candidature of Sir Stuart Donaldson for the representation of Bath. Donaldson permanently returned to England in 1859 and unsuccessfully contested the House of Commons seats of Dartmouth and Barnstaple in 1860.[40] Caroline was obviously not impressed by his campaign speeches, reported in the Sydney papers. She questioned what Donaldson's beliefs were, and reiterated that she believed in the equality of rights, not equality of property; equal rights of protection—perfect equality in the face of the law.

Caroline spoke of her concern of the cases of female seduction, and expressed her hope that some protection might before long be provided by the law for the victims, and that the seducers be punished. She was one of the first in Australia to suggest legislation, other than rape laws, had a role in advancing women's sexual rights.[41]

Caroline then referred to her travels on the European continent, where there had been prejudice against her. Although Caroline had nothing to do with immigration from there, she had found it difficult in France to get her name advertised in connection with Australia. However, once it was known she was in France, many people sought her out to ask her about Australia. The French were of the opinion that 'Napoleon was a good name to fight under, but a bad name to farm under'.

His Holiness, the Pope, had granted Caroline an audience, and he had told her the plough was good—good for women and children, and recommended the plough be preserved in Australia. The Pope had said that railroads were commercial missionaries that nothing could stop; but, with all improvements, let the plough prosper.

The system of what Caroline called 'red-tapeism' upon the railways in Australia obviously upset her. She related how she had been asked nine times for her ticket on her way to Campbelltown. She regretted that after all she had done for the colony the government could not give her free rail travel, as they had done for her in England.

Drawing to a close, she spoke of the progress of democracy in the colony—the democracy of the yearning of man and woman for a home, a home where they might have armchairs for their parents, and rocking cradles for their little children. She said that the women of Australia were brave, and would despise a man who was not ready to defend his country. Once again Caroline impressed upon her audience to read the *Herald* and the *Empire*, and to use their own judgement.

These four lectures show Caroline's strength of character. She did not hesitate to severely criticise the squatters and those in power, and she strongly advocated the power of the woman's role, even to the extent of having the women sitting on the platform overlooking the men below in the auditorium. This could well have been a safety precaution but nonetheless would have given the women a sense of importance. That so many women attended the meetings illustrates how Caroline created an interest in politics and shows that women were not afraid to be seen attending a political lecture. She encouraged women to break with tradition and involve themselves in debates on political affairs, and she sought equality between the sexes by suggesting that men should take their share of the responsibilities of the home. This was thus contrary to the 1960s and 1970s feminists' view of Caroline. They accused her of being part of the establishment, of being anti-feminist, of continuing the nineteenth-century stereotype of the woman's place in the home. She did indeed place single women as servants close to where she knew bachelors were looking for wives, but there were few alternatives for women at that time.

Caroline had never been afraid of airing her views, and she had a remarkable ability of keeping the audience enthralled with her talks for two hours or so, and used humour to great effect. Newspaper reports of her emigration lectures in England and the lectures in Sydney are full of cheers, hear! hears! and laughter. She could work an audience to get her point across. Her eloquent and damning lectures also refute the criticism that she often played down her role and excused her philanthropic endeavours; she often reminded audiences of what she had previously achieved. That Caroline gave these lectures and was not afraid to attack politicians, squatters and clergy of all denominations may well have been one of the reasons why she slipped from view.

Around the time of the lectures, the colony, and Sydney in particular, was facing horrific problems brought about by the vast influx of immigrants following the discovery of gold. The population had more than trebled in the twenty years from 1841 to 1861. A chronic shortage of housing and widespread unemployment caused working-class poverty and a sharp rise in criminal activity. In *Little Joe* Caroline sought to show the public just how desperate the situation was.

From 26 December 1859 until 15 May 1860, eleven chapters of Caroline's novelette *Little Joe* appeared in the *Empire*.[42] *Little Joe* dealt with very similar topics to those of the lectures, namely, the importance of family life, the very dreadful living conditions working classes had to endure, universal suffrage, vote by ballot, payment to members of parliament, early closing of shops and the unlocking of the lands.

The story is a straightforward tale of young Joe Watt, whose father had died and whose mother was about to be sent to the Benevolent Asylum to die. Mrs Brown, a neighbour, adopts young Joe and lovingly brings him up with her own children. Joe falls under the bad influence of Dingy Jack, and is wrongly accused of stealing some money. Joe is a likeable young lad, and is good, kind, thoughtful, caring and intelligent, but deprived of opportunity. Joe befriends the sickly Laura Jeyes after her father asked Joe to kill Laura's pet dog, who was also ill. Towards the end of the serialisation the rich Mr Jeyes comes to understand that there is more to life than work and money. He supports Joe and gets him out of trouble. This is a simple story, told in a natural way. It is not a classic, and Caroline does tend to tell the reader what to think, rather than allow the story to make its own point. However, it is very readable. *Little Joe* was written shortly after Caroline heard of the death of her mother, and there are a number of links to her home life in Northampton. The characteristics of Mrs Brown could well have been reflections of her mother.

In the novelette, Caroline reiterates her belief that the working man should have the chance to obtain land. She believed that this would be advantageous to the country, but that it needed the 'exertion of the people; [for] our system is bad, bad, thoroughly bad, and unless we get vote by ballot, manhood suffrage and payment of members, we can never expect the country to improve'. Little Joe's father died from the hopelessness of having a lease on his property: 'he felt the entanglement of his case, and that all his labour was in a manner thrown away; he sank his money and wasted his time and his strength on a piece of ground so confined that you could hardly turn a horse and cart round in it'. All the money and the labour Mr Watt sank into his leasehold property 'ought to have placed him in possession of a snug farm'.

Caroline had her characters discuss the importance of educating children. Particularly if the children had the misfortune to become orphans, then they should not be allowed, 'like Joe, to be without instruction, without a home, exposed to the plots of designing men.' The actual system of education was debated. As with the school in Madras, Caroline believed children needed to be praised and not censured or harshly punished. Children should be encouraged, stimulated and listened to and treated with respect, not treated with disdain and contempt and made examples of before the whole school. The system in the school that Dingy Jack attended had undermined a boy's health, 'and a nervous excitement was destroying his memory'.

Mr and Mrs Crampton are shown as a loving couple, and the husband pays attention to his wife's needs. 'He had to wait half an hour before his wife could get ready; but the baker knew well that a little time lost in pleasing a wife was a profitable investment of time and money.' Caroline may not have voiced her opinion on the position of women *per se*, but as in her emigration lectures she often referred to the fact that husbands should look after their wives. As previously noted, in a lecture in her home town of Northampton on 5 March 1853, she exclaimed, 'I never can imagine that Almighty God sent females into the world to be cooks and housemaids all their days'.

On religious matters, Caroline wrote of the rule of Sunday observance and the payment for pews in church and left the reader to mull over the injustice of the church being divided by those who could pay a shilling in the front, sixpence in the gallery, or were kept standing in a separated pen, like cattle in the sale yards. Characters in *Little Joe* also discuss the question of state-aid to the clergy. The reader is in no doubt that the author believed that it was 'a grave impediment to true religion in the Colony' and that 'the sooner the blessing [abolishment of state-aid] is brought about, the better', for 'State-aid brings the influence of Government to bear on Ecclesiastical appointments'.

Throughout *Little Joe* Caroline frequently drew attention to the belief that the rich had a duty to the poor, but stated that the 'rich know not the overflowing tenderness of the poor.' It was something that she often voiced: 'he who gives from an overflowing purse comparatively gives but little, to him who gives his mite from a scanty one'.

Caroline's calling her serial *Little Joe* could well have been a salute to Charles Dickens. In *Bleak House* the street-sweeper Jo is moved on so effectively that he is hounded out of London and eventually dies. Appalled by the conditions in which many such street urchins lived and died in London, Charles Dickens interrupted the storyline to appeal to the Queen and the upper classes to do something to help. Likewise, the streets of Sydney were full of Joes, and Caroline wanted the public to do something about it.

During the period of the lectures and writing, Caroline was beset by ill health and financial problems. This prompted her to write to Father Therry for a loan of £15 or £20.[43] The Papal Medal was pawned to help subsidise the family. Some considerable while later, Archibald junior found and purchased the medal.

To help alleviate financial difficulties and educate their young daughters, Caroline and Monica, Caroline opened a school at Rathbone House, Stanmore, and later moved the school to Greenbank, Tempe. Rathbone House was possibly named after the Rathbones of Liverpool, with whom Caroline had become friendly when lecturing in Liverpool in 1853. Greenbank was the name of the Rathbone home in Liverpool. Moving the 'Educational Establishment for Young Ladies' allowed for additional pupils. An advertisement in the *Empire* on 6 July 1863 notes that 'the Rooms of the House are spacious, lofty, and well ventilated, and the out-buildings are excellent'. The property had 'twelve acres of Pleasure Grounds and Gardens attached, with a fine, large, open Orchard of Fruit trees, intersected by wide and shady walks'. There was also 'a good Bath-House adjoining the House, where the Young Ladies will have the further benefit of Sea-Bathing, as often as may be deemed desirable'. Ever practical, Caroline's advertisement notes that 'Buses run from Sydney and Newtown, to within fives minutes walk of Tempe'. This establishment would appear to run counter to the things Caroline had done in the past. This was a school for young ladies rather than for poor young girls. But there was a need to support the family, and, as with the opening of the store, a school carried with it an acceptable social status, and enabled Caroline to earn a livelihood as well as educate her daughters.

The Chisholms had much to celebrate during this period of their lives, and much to regret. William, their second son, married Susanna McSwiney at St Francis Church, Melbourne, on 20 April 1857. Caroline's first grandchild, and William and Susanna's first daughter, Josephine, was born on 18 March 1858. William, however, died quite suddenly in Melbourne in December that year. Josephine died a month later. Susanna Chisholm later joined the Sisters of Charity, where she was noted for her charitable nature, and held the position of Reverend Mother at the convent at Woollahra, NSW.[44] Caroline's mother, Sarah Jones, died on 28 March 1859. The news may have taken some time to reach Caroline and her family in Sydney. Sarah's will states that all her houses, lands, tenements, appurtenances etc. should be sold and divided equally between her five daughters, Charlotte Wright (widow), Mary Ann Auld (widow), Harriet Goode (widow), Sarah Gage (wife of Samuel Gage) and Caroline. There were a number of properties to be sold and the legacy would have been substantial. In view of the financial problems and difficulties of the Chisholm family, there is the question as to whether or not Caroline received it. The legacy may have helped pay for the school that Caroline founded, or for the return fares to England.

To complete the girls' education, Archibald, Sydney, Caroline junior and Monica left Australia for England in 1865. Sydney was twenty, Caroline eighteen and Monica fifteen. Caroline, too ill to travel with the family, remained with Archibald junior. Henry had married Kate Hefferman in Sydney on 13 October 1864 and he often visited Caroline at Archibald's lodgings at 6 O'Connell Street.

Following their arrival in England, Archibald, Sydney, Caroline and Monica spent some time in Liverpool. During June and July 1865 they were often at Greenbank, the home of Elizabeth and William Rathbone, for lunch or dinner.[45] The family also visited Archibald's brother John in Cheltenham.[46] It was in Cheltenham that Caroline junior had a photograph taken for a carte-de-visite. A trip was made to Scotland to visit Archibald's brother Colin, a solicitor living in Inverness with his wife Margaret and several children, aged between seven and twenty-three.

Caroline junior started at the Convent Elm Villa, Highgate, on 20 March 1866. It was run by the Marist Sisters in 'a pretty little house with a garden on Holloway Road at the foot of Highgate Hill and quite a distance from St Joseph's Church on the crown of the hill'.[47] It is believed Monica attended a Belgian convent, but no further details have been found.[48]

Caroline wrote to Elizabeth Rathbone on 22 September 1865. She wrote, 'My Dear Mrs Rathbone, I am sure you will be pleased to hear that I am getting better, every day this last week I have been able to go out for a walk twice a day and find great benefit from doing so; I go out in the morning ¼ to 9 and return at five minutes past—in the cool of the evg I take a slow walk for twenty minutes'.[49]

She still had hopes of being of use to those wishing to emigrate in England. Her letter to Elizabeth Rathbone continued:

> Only yesterday Mr Cowper the Colonial Secretary appraised me that my Pension for £200 per annum for life should be on the Estimates; the House meets in October and before the Xmas holidays the Estimates must pass the House. The Appropriation Bill will follow so that I have every reason to expect I may leave here in January, I should not think of doing so until I had received my first months pension—after seeing Mr Cowper I called on the Minister of Land and Emigration to thank him for his promise of support, and he took that opportunity of assuring me that when I was certain of going home he would like to know that he would see that funds were available to enable me to render service to the colony without injury to myself. [50]

Even in her twilight years, Caroline was as practical as ever. She asked Elizabeth Rathbone if she could find out how much the rent of a house would be near the docks 'to enable me to visit ships and for parties about emigrating to call upon me for information'. Caroline wanted to be fully prepared with all necessary information. Regrettably she did not receive the pension. A search of the parliamentary papers indicates that the appropriation bill was never passed.

Obviously Caroline had high hopes of being able to be of service to the colony. She drafted a notice of the 'Liverpool Committee of Advice In the Protection of Emigrants'. It reads:

> The Committee have no pecuniary interest in emigration, but are willing to afford information and to advise country persons sailing from

Liverpool in the choice of ships—lodgings and etc. on their arrival at Liverpool [the words underlined were deleted].

Also on the recommendation of the Sydney Melbourne & Adelaide Committee to receive instructions regarding Remittances made by Emigrants there to assist their relations (sic relatives) in this country and to see that the sum be properly appropriated.

Committee–Acting Hon. Secy.[51]

Caroline would have been fifty-eight in 1866 and it seems remarkable that she was still hoping to continue her work back in England. This may have been necessary to help pay for the education of the girls and a way of justifying a pension. Perhaps it is also an indication that she was finding it difficult to retire and work was a way of not giving in to illness.

Shortly after her return to England in 1866, and while they were still living in Liverpool, Caroline's name was used for fraudulent purposes. A young man by the name of Henry Phillip Dashwood Arthy was charged at the Bow Street Police Court with having obtained the sum of £100 from the Royal Bounty Fund and with forging the receipt of Mrs Caroline Chisholm.[52] Arthy had written in July 1866 to Prime Minister Lord Derby (the former Lord Stanley) requesting financial assistance in the name of Caroline Chisholm, praying for a grant from the Royal Bounty Fund and pleading poverty and ill-health. The court case necessitated Caroline's attendence at the hearing and giving evidence. This would seem to indicate that Caroline had not been entirely forgotten as her financial situation was known.

Caroline was awarded an annual pension of £100 from the British Government in June 1867. The Rathbones may have been instrumental in obtaining it. An item in Elizabeth's diary for 14 May 1867 reads 'called Mrs Chisholm told her of Pension'.

The last entry in Elizabeth Rathbone's diary that notes she had visited or been called upon by Mrs Chisholm is dated 19 October 1868. The 'Major and Mrs Chisholm' stayed at 15 Brookland Road, Old Swan, Liverpool and at 255 East India Road. There is no further information concerning their stay in Liverpool. What is clear is the close friendship between the two women.

By 1869 Caroline and Archibald were living in London at 3 Great Winchester Buildings, Winchester Street, Highgate Hill, and then 6 Whittington Grove, Highgate. Daughter Caroline remained at home with the family until her marriage to Edmund Gray, the son of Sir John Gray MP, on 13 July 1869. Edmund became the Mayor of Dublin, sole proprietor of *Freeman's Journal* and a member of parliament for Tipperary. His father died in 1875 and left him considerable property. On the night of the census in 1871, only Archibald and Caroline were at home. A Matilda Copner from Warwickshire, Birmingham, and a Margaret U. Kearsy from Wicklow, Ireland, were noted as visiting, but they may have been taken in as lodgers. The Chisholms at that time had a servant, Ann Smith, born in Bethnal Green, Middlesex.

On 21 September 1875 Archibald wrote to their son Henry in Australia from Highgate Hill, London, authorising him to 'receive on my account from any party who possess them, one Gold Medal, and one gold crop'.[53] This was the medal Caroline had received from Pius IX, and on her sickbed she may have been fretting about it. Archibald wrote another note the same day to Henry giving details of his pension from the Madras Military Fund. Archibald, ten years older than his wife, must have worried considerably for her welfare should he die before her, as he suspected he would. Archibald had been subscribing to the Madras Military Fund since he entered the service. After Archibald's death, Caroline would have been entitled to £147.16.0d per year for Monica, while single, and she herself would have received £40 per year. Caroline's own pension, as noted above, was £100 per annum. Archibald's letter to Henry also indicated that if both he and Caroline were dead, then Monica would be allowed £60 a year. If she remained single, then Archibald felt sure that 'friends would make interest with Government, on death of us both, to grant her the yearly pension her mother had, or at least half of it'.[54] Friends did indeed contact the government to seek a pension for Monica on the death of both Archibald and Caroline. Florence Nightingale wrote to her brother-in-law, the MP Sir Harry Verney, on Easter Day (1 April 1877):

> You know that Mrs Chisholm, the Emigrants' friend (and alas Mrs Nassau Senior both) died last week. They are to try to get Mrs Chisholm's pension of £100 continued to her unmarried daughter. Who has nothing (Major Chisholm who still lives having only his pension). Sidney Herbert, had he lived, would have done this. It is greatly to the credit of the Chisholm family that they have literally no fortune – everything was spent in the work. (She died last Sunday in London after a long illness). If you and Lord Houghton thought well to write to Disraeli about the pension, I should think it would be done.[55]

The English Civil List Pensions during the year ended 20 June 1878 granted Monica the sum of £50 in recognition of the services rendered by her mother, 'the Emigrants' Friend'.

With the assistance of Edmund and Caroline Gray, Archibald and Caroline, with their youngest daughter Monica, removed to 43a Barclay Road, Fulham. They had been at Highgate Hill for five years. The property in Fulham was slightly larger and, importantly, it enabled Caroline to have a bed in the bay window; she had been bedridden for some considerable time. On 25 March 1877, she died. Her death certificate indicates that the cause of death was 'senile softening at brain 6 yrs—bronchitis 14 days, certified by R. Pitman LRCP'.

Archibald died a few months later in Rugby on 17 August 1877. The funerals of both Caroline and Archibald were held at the Catholic Cathedral in Northampton. On the tombstone above their joint grave in the Billing Road Cemetery in Northampton are these words: 'Of your charity pray for the repose of the souls of Caroline Chisholm, The Emigrants Friend who died 25 March 1877 aged 67 years and of Archibald Chisholm, Major, 30th Madras Native Infantry, who died 17 August 1877, aged 81 years. R.I.P.' Neither Caroline nor Archibald left a will. They were survived by four of their nine children, Henry, Sydney, Caroline and Monica. Archibald had died in Sydney two years earlier on 30 January 1875.

Caroline's death was only fleetingly reported in the national papers, and the death notice in the *Northampton Herald* of 7 April 1877 even made errors when giving the names of Caroline and Archibald. In the body of the report it states, 'The deceased lady was the daughter of William Jones of Wootton, where the family resided and hence may have arisen the mistake that she was born there. The fact is that she was born in this town, about the year 1808, and married Captain Alex Chisholm of the Madras Army.' The end of the funeral notice, with its unfortunate error, reads, 'It is intended to raise by mutual subscription, a monument to her memory, in which movement we are sure the townspeople will join, for no Cemetery contains a more honoured grave than that of Mrs Catherine Chisholm.'

Photograph of the Gravestone of Caroline and Archibald in the Billing Road Cemetery, Northampton. (The upkeep of the grave has now been taken over by the Caroline Chisholm School in Northampton.)

OF YOUR CHARITY PRAY FOR
THE REPOSE OF THE SOULS

OF

CAROLINE CHISHOLM

The Emigrants Friend,

Who Died 25th March 1877,

Aged 67 Years,

and of

ARCHIBALD CHISHOLM

Major, 30th Madras

Native Infantry,

Who died 17th August 1877,

Aged 81 Years.

R.I.P

AFTERWORD

The Biographies and their Authors

Samuel Sidney was an ardent supporter of emigration, but wrote articles on Caroline rather than a memoir. He was born Samuel Solomon in Birmingham in 1813, the son of a well-known surgeon. He studied law and became a solicitor before turning to a life of journalism, changing his name from Solomon to Sidney. His brother John lived in Australia from 1838 to 1844, and it is through his reports that Sidney became fascinated with the colony. Sidney himself never visited Australia. His emigration publications included *Sidney's Emigrant Journal*, published weekly between October 1848 and July 1849, and *Sidney's Australian Handbook*, published in 1848 and reprinted nine times by November 1849. Sidney's *Emigrant's Journal and Traveller's Magazine* was produced monthly for six months during 1849 and 1850, and he published a 400-page volume entitled *The Three Colonies of Australia* in 1853. Many of Sidney's contributions to *Household Words*[1] were concerned with emigration and these were successfully reprinted in 1854 under the title of *Gallops and Gossips in the Bush of Australia*, which was dedicated to Charles Dickens. In 1851 Sidney was appointed assistant commissioner for the Great Exhibition. Sidney also took a keen interest in agriculture and equine concerns and was hunting correspondent for the *Illustrated London News* from 1847 to 1857. *The Book of the Horse*, published in 1873, was his most important work. He died in 1883.[2]

Sidney is eulogistic of Caroline. In Sidney's *Emigrant's Journal and Traveller's Magazine*, August 1849, he writes:

> The distinguishing characteristic of Mrs Chisholm is philanthropy—extending to all classes and all sects—directed by a degree of common sense that almost amounts to genius, united with an energy, a zeal, an untiring perseverance that renders nothing she undertakes impossible.
>
> Her philanthropy is not a mere amusement to be taken up at odd hours, like a new romance—to be laid down as quickly as it was taken up—to be satisfied by a distribution of cheap tracts, or, at most, of cheap superfluous guineas—by capricious visits to poor cottages, whose misery renders the change from the luxurious drawing-room a pleasing excitement. It is a part of her life—of her daily duty. For the cause she embraced she has chosen to abandon the luxuries, nay, the comforts, to which her fortune and station entitled her; to wear stuff instead of silk; to work hard, to live hard, to save, that she may spend upon her poor.
>
> Thousands have reason to bless Mrs Chisholm. We find her not like Mrs Fry—descending from the drawing-room to the prison, to return, carriage-borne, to that drawing-room, when her errand of mercy was done—but in the small room of a small house, in an obscure suburb, writing at a rickety table, amid piles of colonial documents, answers to her thousand correspondents'.[3]

Sidney was not so impressed by the work of Hannah More and her distribution of 'cheap tracts'. More faced criticism for her educational programme and her belief that it was a 'cruelty and not [a] kindness to educate people above their station in life'.[4] Neither was Sidney impressed by the philanthropy of ladies who distribute 'cheap superfluous guineas—by capricious visits to poor cottages, whose misery renders the change from the luxurious drawing room a pleasing excitement'. Sidney was also not impressed by Mrs Fry and her work at Newgate Prison, from which she would return, in the comfort of her carriage, to the luxury of her comfortable home.

Sidney cannot understand why tears are wept 'when a millionaire endows a church or founds a hospital', which involves no self-sacrifice whatsoever, yet 'a head and heart that might with happiness to the world found and govern a colonial empire, toils and moils over the petty economy of household details in order to save for her poor emigrants'. He wonders why Caroline and 'her noble-minded husband', who had refused any 'pecuniary compensation for their sacrifices', had not been 'offered some signal mark of regard for so much wisdom and virtue combined'. He compares the lack of acknowledgement of Caroline's work to the knighthood that Charles Trevelyan received, 'together with a bonus of a few thousands sterling', for a year's hard work at his duty in Ireland. Sidney is very direct in his opinion that Caroline's work should be officially recognised.[5]

The *ILN* wrote a glowing report of *The Three Colonies of Australia* in its issue of 6 November 1852: 'It is beautifully illustrated and speaks to the eye, no less than to the mind'. At six shillings a copy, however, it was not a book for the poor. The report commented upon the 'delightful' chapter on Mrs Chisholm with an 'account of her disinterested and noble exertions, together with some amusing and graphic notes of her own. Everyone, who knew it not already, can see that she not only possesses an excellent heart, but that she is also a person of extraordinary fortitude, and a most enlightened understanding. She well deserves the title of protectress of the unfortunate and defender of the poor.'

There have been different versions of Caroline and Archibald's meeting with the Highland emigrants and the help that they gave them. In his *Journal* in 1849 Sidney suggests that it was Caroline who helped the Highland emigrants, as did Eneas Mackenzie writing in 1852. Sidney, writing in 1853 in *The Three Colonies of Australia*, notes that Archibald initiated the help (had Caroline read the *Journal* and corrected it?). Eleanor Dark does not relate the tale, whereas Margaret Swann states that Captain Chisholm lent the Highlanders money to purchase tools.[6] Margaret Kiddle merely notes that the 'Chisholms met some Highlanders'.[7] Mary Hoban greatly extends the incident to several paragraphs, suggesting Archibald originally became involved with the Highlanders and was about to give them some money when Caroline suggested that part of the money should be expended on ropes and equipment to enable them to become woodcutters.[8] Joanna Bogle follows Mary Hoban's description of the incident as if it was a true fact and does not take into account Hoban's declared biographical fictionalisation.[9]

Sidney was more of a friend to Caroline than Mackenzie. He was named as such by the *ILN* when he attended a farewell meeting for her before her return to Australia[10] on the *Ballarat* on 10 April 1854. He was also involved with the *FCLS* and would deputise for Mrs Chisholm at emigration meetings. Sidney himself confessed his friendship and indebtedness to the Chisholms, to whose friendship he attributed his 'great and rapid advance in which I may call my colonial education'.[11] As Assistant Commissioner for the Great Exhibition in 1851 he may well have been instrumental in the organisation of Caroline's visit, during the first three days of the exhibition, with the *FCLS* emigrants just before their departure on the *Blundell* for Australia on 10 May 1851.[12]

Sidney's praise perpetuated the Victorian ideological view of womanhood: he put Caroline on a pedestal. Although originally a supporter of the Wakefield system of colonisation and land monopoly, Sidney became an ardent believer that 'land monopoly was the great bar to the popularity of Australia among the working classes'.[13] He attacked Wakefield's colonial land monopoly in print and at public meetings, and was for a time excluded from any part of the Colonisation Society of Charing Cross, of which he was a member.[14]

Eneas Mackenzie followed Sidney's style of writing, but is far more flamboyant. Mackenzie was the first to write a memoir of Chisholm, and it was written in her lifetime. Mackenzie's work was entitled *Memoirs of Mrs Caroline Chisholm, with an account of her Philanthropic labours, in India, Australia and England. To which is added a History of the Family Colonisation Loan Society, with its Rules, Regulations, and Pledges. Also the question answered who ought to Emigrate. The Emigrant's Guide to Australia with a Memoir of Mrs Chisholm (Emigrant's Guide)* was published by Mackenzie in London in 1853. Little can be traced of Mackenzie himself. His father, also Eneas, a strong radical and Secretary of the Northern Political Union, founded the printing and publishing firm of Mackenzie and Dent, which published works to be sold in periodical parts. Eneas senior gave up his Presbyterian faith to join the Baptists, was an ardent social reformer and political agitator and principal founder of the Newcastle Literary, Scientific and Mechanical Institute in 1824.[15] He obviously had a considerable influence upon his son, Caroline's biographer.[16]

Eneas junior did not continue with the profitable publications of his father's company. He started a radical newspaper, *The Newcastle Press*, in 1832. The motto of the paper was 'Liberty and Equality ... Universal Suffrage: Annual Parliaments; and Vote by Ballot'. The paper collapsed because of labour difficulties and ceased publication in the summer of 1834. Mackenzie purchased the Newcastle circulating library from the radical printer John Marshall when he became bankrupt in 1831. The library had been badly managed before Mackenzie's purchase, but he soon re-established it and 9,000 volumes were listed in 1832. By 1833 he had handed over the running of the library to his mother, Elizabeth, prior to his emigration to Australia in 1834.[17] Mackenzie returned to England in 1845, a year before the Chisholms, where he wrote guides for Australian emigrants and published educational books.[18]

Mackenzie's *Memoirs* were written as an exemplar. At that time history was written from the male, public and military perspective, making the domestic of little interest. The public and personal were kept well apart, especially where women were concerned. The achievement of the subject was what mattered, not the 'minute personal illustration'. In the kind of society in which Mackenzie lived, 'girls learned early in life that they were less important than boys'.[19] Mackenzie was also aware that Caroline had been the victim of some 'ungentlemanly' intrusion into her personal life, and this may well have made him more hesitant in revealing minute personal illustrations and he therefore 'attended more to positive public facts'. Mackenzie's words and his stance were very much in accord with the 'belief in biography as a moral force capable of changing the lives of its readers', which was influential in the 1850s.[20]

The words Mackenzie uses to bring the *Memoir* to a close leave us in no doubt as to his views on Caroline. He believed that she had a 'God-like mission'. Although Caroline had moved out of the private realm of the home and into the public sphere, to Mackenzie she was still continuing the 'domestic, social and intellectual virtues' that the Victorians so admired in their women. While he put her on a pedestal, at the same time he kept her firmly in her place: subservient to the male. Mackenzie's acclaim for Caroline in 'protecting the weak and sheltering the poor' is seen as an extension of her female role of protecting and sheltering her family. These are virtues that he wished to be admired and imitated. Mackenzie's radicalism, encapsulated in the motto of his Newcastle paper, show that he would have wished for others to emulate her ardent support for moral and social reform.

Mackenzie's *Emigrant's Guide* continues the same underlying tone: 'Health, decency and morality are now provided for in a manner heretofore unknown ... The instrument, in God's hands, of this moral reformation is CAROLINE CHISHOLM.'[21] The memoir of Mrs Chisholm in the *Emigrant's Guide* is an essay of thirty-two pages. It gives advice as to who should emigrate, information on the different emigration societies, the choice of ship and so on. Caroline wrote a chapter of advice on 'Outfits' and a short section on 'Bush Cookery'.

It had originally been intended that *Memoirs* was to be a serialised publication. While Mackenzie apologised for any 'slight errors in style, arrangement or typography that may have escaped' his notice 'in passing through the press',[22] it is unforgivable of him not to have corrected the misnaming of Caroline's husband as 'Alexander'. This error was repeated twenty-five years later in Caroline's obituary in the *ILN*.

Perhaps because of Mackenzie's wish not to 'lift the veil' on his subject's personal life, there are discrepancies in the *Memoirs* and *The Emigrant's Guide* in the few details he gives of Caroline's birth, in particular her birthplace. These have been reiterated in successive biographies of Caroline until they have almost become established fact. A few local historians in Northamptonshire would rather believe previously written biographies rather than accept new evidence that establishes Caroline's birthplace as Northampton.

Patricia Grimshaw, writing an introduction to the reprint of Kiddle's biography in 1990, suggested that Mackenzie 'knew Caroline well, as a member of her Colonisation Society, and was acquainted with many of her friends'. He was no doubt aware of Caroline and her work in Sydney before he returned to England in 1845, as there were numerous reports of her work in the Sydney newspapers. I can find no trace, however, of a friendship between Caroline and Mackenzie prior to his involvement with the *FCLS* in 1850.[23] In the Preface to *Memoirs* Mackenzie thanks Samuel Sidney 'for many facts which he generously placed at our disposal'[24] and talks of his 'investigations of the facts placed before the public'.[25] If Mackenzie had known Caroline that well he would not have had to rely upon Sidney's facts, and would have known that her husband was Archibald and not Alexander, and his work would not have contained some muddled or ambiguous information.

Samuel Smiles, whose work *Self-Help* was published in 1859, was one of the most influential of Victorian popular biographers. He preached the benefits of independence, energy, industry and thrift, promising readers that it was in their power to improve their lot. Exemplary lives were an important part of his philosophy.[26] Samuel Smiles, under the chapter heading of 'Example – Models', referred to Caroline's life and work. He wrote of Mrs Chisholm's remarks to Mrs Stowe on the secret of her success. 'I found', Caroline said, 'that if we want anything *done*, we must go to work and *do*: it is of no use merely to talk—none whatever'. Smiles continues:

> It is poor eloquence that only shows how a person can talk. Had Mrs Chisholm rested satisfied with lecturing, her project, she was persuaded, would never have got beyond the region of talk; but when people saw what she was doing and had actually accomplished, they fell in with her views and came forward to help her. Hence the most beneficent worker is not he who says the most eloquent things, or even who thinks the most loftily, but he who does the most eloquent acts.[27]

Smiles was obviously impressed that Caroline did not just talk, but got on with things and actually got her hands dirty doing the work.

The biographers writing between the mid-nineteenth century and before Kiddle's work in the mid-twentieth century tended to write shorter biographies and articles and in the main drew heavily upon the information in Mackenzie's *Memoirs*.

Trelawney Saunders of Charing Cross published a small biography in London in 1852. *The Story of the Life of Mrs Caroline Chisholm, The Emigrants' Friend, and her adventures in Australia* was priced at one penny and would have been readily available to intending emigrants. The pamphlet used material from *Sidney's Emigrant's Journal* (second series), Caroline's own report of the emigrants' home in Sydney, the Blue Books on colonisation issued in New South Wales, and the debates on Irish colonisation before the House of Lords. The pamphlet was written to answer the question 'Who is Mrs Chisholm?' The answer given is that:

> [she] is a lady who is not rich, or related to any great people; but she has been engaged nearly all her life in helping labouring and poor people, by teaching them how to help themselves: and she has succeeded so well, that there are thousands who look upon her with feelings of as much affection as if she were their mother.[28]

The tone of the writing and the price of the pamphlet indicate that it was probably aimed at the poorer end of the market. Saunders, like Mackenzie, Sidney and Smiles, sees Caroline's work as an 'aspirational ideal' but it does not offer the fulsome eulogy of Mackenzie.

By the 1900s 'biography had become more intimate, more concerned with fashionable Freudian psychology'.[29] In a new book (published in 2008) detailing the *Historical Accounts of Caroline Chisholm and her Work*, titled *Unfeigned Love*, Rodney Stinson[30] draws our attention to three articles from the *Catholic Press*, a transcript of a lecture by Miss Fitzsimmons called *The Influence of Women* and a short piece from *The Tablet*[31] that were published together as *Caroline Chisholm 'The Emigrant's Friend', A Great Catholic Woman* by Wood Printing Works in Dublin circa 1909. Stinson makes the valid and important point that Caroline's Catholic faith is not cited in earlier biographies: she is referred to as Christian and mention is made of her Christian work. The stigma of Catholicism could well account for this. Caroline, in her *Account of the Sydney Immigrants' Home*, does not mention her own faith although she talks openly of her impression that 'God had, in a peculiar manner, fitted me for this work', and that 'during the season of Lent … on the Easter Sunday, I was enabled, at the Alter of our Lord, to make an offering of my talents to the God who gave them, and I promised to know *neither country nor creed*, but to serve all justly and impartially'.

The *Catholic Press* article does not contain the exaggerated flowery eulogistic wording of Mackenzie's *Memoirs* but follows a similar line of Mackenzie's work up until the 1850s. As Stinson suggests, there are 'flourishes' of local interest and later information, and the article concludes by drawing a picture of Caroline as another 'Lady with the Lamp'. Stinson suggests that the Fitzsimmons' lecture is "simply a period piece … in what may be the first such portrayal, it places Caroline among a complete array of illustrious women who were Christian activists, identifies some of her qualities that are worthy of emulation and asks that the Catholic Women's League 'claim this great and noble woman as our very own'". Stinson includes the article in *The Tablet* merely because it was in the Irish booklet, not because of its reliability.[32] It notes that Caroline was a 'Scottish lady'. The short article comments on Caroline's advocacy of the 'Ocean penny postage, as well as of the money-order system; while her school for the training of soldiers' wives and orphans at Madras (which still exists) served in many respects as the model on which the industrial and technical training schools were afterwards formed'.

Edith Pearson, writing in 1914, included a short essay on Caroline in her collection of essays and poems in *Ideals and Realities*. In line with her interests in ideals, the first chapter starts with a quotation from Carlyle: 'For human things do require to have an Ideal in them'. Pearson also quotes Carlyle at the head of the chapter on Caroline: 'Labour, wide as the earth, has its summit in Heaven'.[33] It is easy to speculate that Pearson was perhaps harking back to the earlier biographical form, but her chatty essay recounts information supplied by Caroline's daughter Caroline, with whom Pearson had spoken, and the essay peers behind the veil of domestic life. It clearly shows Pearson as spiritually minded. Although her essay contains minor inaccuracies, she imparts details of Caroline's private life that are not found in other biographies. Some details have been substantiated, while others have been difficult either to prove or disprove. It is the first time that the story of William Jones's befriending a maimed soldier appears in print.

The work of G. Elliot Anstruther, Organising Secretary of the Catholic Truth Society, was published in England in 1916, as part of the 'Women-Workers' series, priced at one penny.[34] Anstruther's work draws upon articles in the *ILN*, *The Westminster Review*, and *Chamber's Journal* as well as the works that Caroline herself had written. This is a very short biographical work and, as one would expect, it mentions Caroline's religious beliefs. Anstruther makes clear, however, that her 'philanthropic undertakings, were far from the spirit of proselytism'.[35] The brief biography is in line with the new biographical approach in that it is more intimate and talks of Caroline's birth and early years, but the concluding paragraphs hark back to the eulogistic approach with references to Michelet's[36] reference to Mrs Chisholm as Australia's 'saint' and 'legend'.

As far as can be ascertained the above are the last biographical sketches that were written in the United Kingdom prior to Margaret Kiddle's work in 1950. The Australian biographers before Kiddle were Margaret Swann and Eleanor Dark. Swann was interested in local history and was at one time President of the Parramatta Historical Society. She gave a lecture to the Royal Australian Historical Society on the subject of Caroline in 1919, and produced her 75-page book, *Caroline Chisholm – Friend to the Unemployed and Migrants, New South Wales and Victoria 1838 to 1866*, in 1925.

As in Caroline's lifetime, in 1925 the want of labour in Australia was desperate. Swann, as Grimshaw rightly suggests, 'was clearly impressed with a specifically Australian reading of Caroline's work'.[37] She felt it 'only natural that we [Australia] should extend a hearty welcome to the surplus population of the Motherland when they come to found homes upon our shores ... in the vast unpopulated tracts in Australia'.[38] Swann was concerned that Australia was rich in everything that goes to make 'wealth and prosperity, except the one essential element—labour'. Australia needed labour to develop its resources, and 'the welcome [Australia] gives [the immigrants] is a very practical one, for everything possible is done to smooth their way, and to guide them until they become accustomed to their new surroundings'.[39] Swann reiterates Caroline's own words in a letter to the Sydney press in July 1862 in which she states: 'The great want of this country ... is population. We want a body of people to develop the great resources of this country ... What mind can contemplate such a country as this ... immense tracts of uncultivated land ... without painfully reverting to his suffering, starving country people at home, to wish that they were here.'[40] Swann is impressed with Caroline's encouragement of self-help: 'Do not ... ask what will the Government do for us? but let your question be: 'What shall we do for ourselves.'[41]

Swann was not alone in being impressed with Caroline's encouragement of self-help, and Caroline's words remind us today of Kennedy's famous quotation in his inaugural address on 20 January 1961. 'Fellow Americans: ask not what your country can do for you, ask what you can do for your country. My fellow citizens of the world: ask not what America will do for you but what together we can do for the freedom of the man.' The quotation originated from the work of Oliver Wendell Holmes, senior, 1809–1894. He founded the *Atlantic Monthly* with J. R. Lowell in 1857.

Swann significantly details at some length Caroline's political lectures in Sydney in the late 1850 and 60s and is impressed by her public works. She highlights the fact that Caroline often felt called upon to justify her right to speak at lectures and to write to men in power. Swann considered that Caroline was attacking the ideology of the time whereby a woman had no right to enter public politics. She defended Caroline against an attack by a member of the audience at an 1852 meeting of the NSW Legislative Council who argued that a 'woman should use her housekeeping talents only'. Swann suggested that the 'speaker did not realise that it was her very womanliness and motherliness which prompted Mrs Chisholm to sacrifice her own comfort in order to accomplish such tasks as the protection of women and children, the reunion of separated families, and similar work'.[42] At the same time, Swann understood that Caroline's firm belief in her right to address an audience on emigration, and to write to men in power on the subject, challenged the Victorian idea of woman's place being the private world of the home.

Eleanor Dark was a woman of literary talent. She was born in Sydney in 1901 and published her first collection of poems at the age of twenty. In 1936 she won the Australian Literary Society's Gold Medal for her *Return to Coolami*. She was concerned with issues of social justice and many of her novels were about the meaning of democracy and the motivation for war. Sexual and racial politics were also the subject of much of her fiction.[43] Dark contributed an essay on Caroline to *The Peaceful Army: A Memorial to the Pioneer Women of Australia 1788 to 1938*. The book was published to celebrate Australia's sesquicentenary in 1938 and was written specifically to give credit to the contribution that women had made to the development of the country and the culture.[44] Dark, like Swann, wanted to see Caroline's work historically accepted. She was obviously impressed by Caroline's work and the fact that she stepped outside the realms of the private sphere. Dark wrote, 'not half a dozen books by Mary Wollstonecraft could have been more effective "vindication" than the life of this indomitable woman'.[45] This view stands in stark contrast to that of Australian feminists of the 1960s and 70s who attacked Caroline's actions for contributing to the low self-esteem suffered by Australian women in the later half of the twentieth century.

Eleanor Dark's work shows the advancing techniques of biographical studies. Dark's chapter puts Caroline back into context. It may be rather brief, but Dark gives us an understanding of the background of Caroline's life. Dark is aware that 'absorbing as the bare record of [Caroline's] almost superhuman endeavours and achievements must always remain, she has a new importance and a new significance when considered in relation to her times'.[46] Dark saw Caroline as one who 'saw evils she could redress, she saw suffering she could allay, she saw despair and bitterness which she could dispel'. She had difficulty with the idea that Caroline was a role model who symbolised female freedom from social conventions and the contemporary views of her own social environment.

Margaret Kiddle's work *Caroline Chisholm*, published in Australia in 1950, is highly regarded, and rightly so. Kiddle commenced her Masters thesis at Melbourne University before World War II and was not able to complete it until 1947. For the duration of the war Kiddle worked in the public service and in the teaching profession. From 1946 until her death in 1958 she was initially employed as a tutor, and then as senior tutor, in the History Department of Melbourne University. Kiddle wrote children's literature and another significant historical study, *Men of Yesterday: A Social History of the Western District of Victoria*, which was published after her death in 1961.

Kiddle's was the first full-length narrative biography of Caroline's life that had been meticulously researched. Kiddle placed Caroline's life and work in the context of political and economic immigration and settlement of Australia. The fact that her biography was a scholarly work, however, limited its readership. Anne Summers argued in her *Damned Whores and God's Police* that such scholarly work is one within an academic environment that is beyond the reach of the general reader. Summers believed that there was a 'double standard of writing and criticism ... which ensured that a vicious circle exists', and went on to comment that by readers at large 'biographies about women were seldom taken seriously, and certainly not in the way that a political biography of a male politician or some other prominent man is'. Summers felt that biographers of women tended to internalise this, and therefore they offered an excess of chatty, discursive books about Australian women, reinforcing the practice of not taking biographies of women seriously.[47]

As with Dark, Kiddle was aware of the concerns of the woman's role and gender relations both in the 1950s and the mid-nineteenth century, the period of Caroline's work. Kiddle was concerned as to why Caroline, faced with the prejudices she had to overcome as a woman in the mid-nineteenth century, did not move forward to an understanding of the wider issues behind the restrictions on, and the lack of opportunities for, women of her class. Kiddle appreciated that the massive amount of time Caroline spent on her work would not have left much for such questioning, and accepted that Caroline was no rebel or theorist.

Patricia Grimshaw noted that Kiddle did 'not proceed to analyse the meaning of Caroline's agenda for poorer single women, namely, their movement into household service and then into matrimony'.[48] Kiddle supported Sir Keith Hancock's premise that Caroline 'established the dignity of womanhood and the family in New South Wales'.[49] Interpreting Caroline's work in this manner, she suggested that Caroline 'altered the attitude of the community to female immigration, and by fostering family life, she raised the social standard of the whole colony'.[50] It is true that Caroline did not actively seek equality with men, but neither did she believe that 'Almighty God sent females into the world to be cooks and housemaids all their days'.[51]

Kiddle's work is not the glowing, gushing admiration of Mackenzie and Sidney. She found 'Caroline's work constructive, positive and effective'. Her book is a 'careful commentary on Caroline's work as a reformer, as an advocate for poor women and for parents of young children'.[52] But, as Grimshaw notes, the judgements Kiddle makes throughout the biography reveal her own world—that of a middle-class woman brought up in the 1920s and 30s. Her approach is narrative and chronological in style and only limited space is given to a discussion of the influences on, and motivations of, Caroline, or of the success of her work and the prejudices of historians who ignored her achievements.

As Kiddle's biography revealed her own world, so too does the work of the Australian feminists of the 1960s and 1970s. Suggestions of Caroline's 'essential conservatism' reveal the attempts to link her placement of single women in employment near single men to conceptions of women in

Australian society. The twentieth-century feminists create their own anti-feminist Caroline Chisholm to explain attitudes towards women within their own society, tending to ignore the historical context of Caroline and her work. They also ignored the fact that Caroline stepped outside the stereotype of her day.

Mary Hoban, who was born at Kyneton (where the Chisholms once lived), viewed Caroline's work differently. She studied Australian history at the University of Melbourne and later taught in secondary schools before her marriage and life at Kilmore, where she continued her interest in the subject. She was a member of the Historical Commission and sponsor of the Canonisation Cause for Caroline.

Hoban's *Fifty-One Pieces of Wedding Cake*, published in 1973 and republished in 1984 with the title, *Caroline Chisholm – A Biography, Fifty-One Pieces of Wedding Cake*, is very different in style to that of Kiddle. Hoban aimed to include 'more details of human interest' and to 'present Caroline's thinking expressed in her own language' as a way 'towards the recognition she deserves from the Australian nation and the Christian church'.[53] Hoban consciously decided to fictionalise 'Caroline's thinking' within the historical biography. Hoban also chose to distance herself, as Grimshaw notes, 'from the secular radical feminism that was shaking accepted views of femininity in Australia in the early 1970s'.[54]

Religious intent is clearly stated at the commencement of Hoban's biography. She remarks that she hopes 'that it may take [Caroline] one step further on the way towards the recognition she deserves from the Australian nation and the Christian church'. Hoban does not hide her Catholicism or the fact that she was a sponsor for the cause for canonisation of Caroline

Chisholm. Delegates at the Australian Conference of Catholic Laity, held in Sydney in April 1976, asked the Bishops of Australia to consider the cause for Caroline Chisholm. The Bishops' Conference authorised a prayer that could be said for the furtherance of the cause, and Hoban included the prayer in the Australian Catholic Truth Society publication of her short biography of Caroline published in July 1977.

Hoban's sponsorship and support of Caroline's cause went hand in hand with her wish for wider recognition of Caroline's work. The role of 'founding mother', as Hoban remarks, 'was freely acknowledged in her lifetime'. Hoban is quick to use the quotations from Henry Parkes' newspaper the *Empire* in 1859, which claimed that: 'If Captain James Cook discovered Australia ... if John Macarthur planted the first seeds of its extraordinary prosperity ... If Ludwig Leichhardt penetrated and explored its before unknown interior—Caroline Chisholm has done more; she has peopled ... she alone has colonised it in the true sense of the term'. Hoban's works on Caroline demonstrate her 'goodness', her 'saintliness'. In terms of academic research, however, as Grimshaw indicated, Hoban's biography 'had little impact on academic attitudes'.[55]

Hoban's biography was first published in Australia in 1973. That she was working at such a distance from Northampton, England, without the benefits of modern technology, probably accounts for her misrepresentation of the witnesses of William Jones's will. Hoban leads the reader to believe that Mr Penfold and 'two abbés' witnessed the will; that William was not well enough to sign his name and so put his mark and that Caroline was distressed by the thought that her father was unable to do the things he wanted.[56] It is quite clear from William Jones's will that the witnesses were Rob. Abbey and Geo. Abbey and Wm Pinfold (or

Penfold). Directories for Northamptonshire show that Robt. Abbey and Geo. Abbey were attorneys in Gold Street, Northampton. George Abbey was coroner for the county and secretary to the Northamptonshire Law Society by 1830.[57] William Jones did indeed make his mark on the will but this was because he could not write his name, not because he was ill. The suggestion that Robert and George Abbey were abbés is mistaken. Without correction it would be very easy for succeeding biographers to use this information, believing it to be correct.[58]

The first biography to be published in the United Kingdom was by Joanna Bogle, in 1993. The book is disappointing. Bogle is a journalist, author and broadcaster and her biography *Caroline Chisholm—The Emigrant's Friend* is only 157 pages in length, has no index, and is written in a chatty style. Like Hoban, she is a Roman Catholic, and is concerned with Caroline's 'goodness'. Bogle considers briefly some of the values and standards of family life that Caroline advocated. She reflects that Caroline's encouragement of people to have 'faith in their own courage, resilience, independence of spirit, and desire to succeed' is the sort of 'far-sighted acceptance of the potential of the human spirit' that is very much needed today.[59] Bogle's bibliography includes two works, those of Kiddle and Hoban, although she does refer to Mackenzie's work in one of her few footnotes. There is evidence of new research, but there are some minor errors—'the Reverend B. Winthrop', Bogle wrote, was a Roman Catholic priest, when in fact he was the Anglican Vicar of the Church of the Holy Sepulchre at the time of Caroline's marriage in December 1830. On the whole the book adds little to the debate. It has, however, brought Caroline to the attention of a limited public in Britain and Australia.

The Biographer's Dilemma

In writing this book, I have had the same difficulty as others in deciding what material should be used or discarded. Some of the documentation is of such a fascinating nature it is detailed below for the reader's consideration. Various interpretations of the material are possible, but corroborative evidence is thin.

The wording of William Jones's will leaves the reader wondering why Robert and Caroline, the youngest son and daughter, the fifth and seventh child from William's fourth marriage, are chosen at the beginning of the will. Robert was to receive 'all that my close or inclosed ground with the appurtenances situate and being near Castle Hills'.[60] Caroline was to receive 'all that my messuage or tenement with the appurtenances situate standing and being in Bearward Street … now or late in the tenure or occupation of my son William Jones'. Later the will refers to 'the said last mentioned premises [in the Mayorhold] unto and equally between my five children by my said wife, namely Charlotte, Thomas, Mary Ann, Sarah and Harriet'. Harriet was the sixth child from the marriage. Robert and Caroline could have been selected as they were favourite children. Specific properties may have been left to them as a way of ensuring that, should Sarah Jones remarry, her new husband, under the Married Woman's Property Act, would not be entitled to claim those properties left to Caroline and Robert.

Caroline's baptismal record reads 'Caroline, daughter of Sarah and William Jones'. Research shows that this is an unusual form of registering the baptism. For the other children of William Jones, including Robert, baptism records state: 'son/daughter of William and his respective wife, either Elizabeth, Mary, Mary or Sarah Jones'. The officiating officer may have been distracted when he was writing, but nonetheless the registration is in a rare form. Studies of the records show that the normal form is to record the father's Christian name, then the mother's first name, and then the surname.

The 1851 census return for Islington lists Caroline Chisholm as head occupant at 3 Charlton Crescent, London. (At the time of the census Archibald was at sea returning to Australia.) Sarah Laws is recorded, and the entry reads, in relation to the head, 'Mother, widow, aged eighty-four, landed proprietor, born in Nottingham'. The name 'Laws' is written quite clearly, and it is not a corrupted writing of 'Jones'. The 1851 census return for St Sepulchre's parish records Sarah Jones, aged eighty-one, living at the family property of 11 Mayorhold, Northampton. Under the column for 'occupation' she is also given as 'landed proprietor'. In view of the will and Caroline's baptismal record, exhaustive researches were undertaken to establish the validity or otherwise of the Islington and Northampton census returns. They was not merely dismissed as fundamental errors by the enumerators.

An alternative reading could be the possibility that Caroline was fostered out to Sarah Laws, but was the child of Sarah Jones. It was not an uncommon occurrence during the Victorian period for a child to be given to a widow to help her overcome her bereavement. Rarely were such arrangements legally recorded. Sarah Jones had produced seven children in the space of nearly fifteen-and-a-half years—late December 1792 to late May 1808. She may have welcomed the opportunity for her youngest to be brought up by another woman. Edith Pearson relates information given to her by Caroline's daughter Caroline who remembered her mother telling her that as a small child:

> when living with an aged lady in Northampton, a burglar got into the house. Both little girl and old lady heard him and got up. When they came out of their room he was at the foot of the staircase, they on the top. The child immediately, with the presence of mind of a grown person, thought of a bunk of picked coal on the landing, and the little creature, assisted by the old woman, showered down on the surprised marauder, with all the force they had, great lumps of coal.[61]

The recollection shows the quick-wittedness and bravery of the young Caroline Jones, but it is also significant in that it would seem to indicate that Caroline lived with someone other than her family. Caroline's novelette *Little Joe* is concerned with young Joe being brought up by a neighbour following his father's death and his mother's illness, necessitating the mother being taken to the Benevolent Asylum (where she later dies).

The primary sources could be interpreted in other ways. Caroline could be the illegitimate daughter of Sarah Laws and William Jones, hence the baptismal record 'Caroline, daughter of Sarah and William Jones'. A widow Laws was registered in the Poor Rate Book of St Sepulchre's parish church as living in the Mayorhold. Is this why Caroline was selected from the other children from the marriage to Sarah Jones, née Allum, in her father's will? The will of Sarah Jones definitely includes Caroline Chisholm as one of her five daughters. Sarah Jones died in 1859. Caroline was by this time a very well known woman. The announcement of the wedding of Archibald Chisholm and Caroline Jones in the *Northampton Mercury* reads: 'Caroline, youngest daughter of the late William Jones'. It does not give the mother's name.

However the marriage of Caroline's sister, Harriet, also states that she is the 'daughter of the late Mr Jones, of this place'. Presumably this was common practice and of no significance.

Another alternative is that Sarah Laws was paid to educate Caroline and took her into her home to do so. Caroline seems to have been educated above the standards of her brothers and sisters, and half-brothers and sisters, who tended to be trades people. William Jones's will states that 'my said wife and my said Brother (if they shall think proper) or the survivor of them to pay and advance any sum or sums of money for the putting and placing and apprentice or otherwise advancing any or either of my said five children in the world as they shall think fit'. Again William is referring to Charlotte, Thomas, Mary Ann, Sarah and Harriet, but Caroline's mother and uncle may well have thought it fit to advance a sum for Caroline's education. This is, of course, supposition, and the entries in the census returns may well have been coincidental errors on the part of the enumerators.

Caroline's Surviving Children

Of the children from the marriage of Caroline and Archibald Chisholm, four survived their parents. Baby Caroline died at three weeks old in 1831, and Sarah died shortly after her birth in 1850. William died in Australia in December 1858. Archibald junior died in Sydney in 1875. Archibald married Anne Loder and they had two daughters, Caroline and Jean. His wife Anne also died in 1875. Of the surviving children, Henry John married Kate Hefferman on 13 October 1864 and had six children: William John, Mary Ellen, Archibald Frank, Henry Sydney, Edmund Arthur and Caroline. Henry became an army officer and magistrate. Sydney married

Anne Loder's sister Isabella. They did not have any children. Caroline's daughter Caroline married Edmund Dwyer Gray and had four children, Edmund, Mary, Monica and Archibald. Mary entered a convent in Ireland. Edmund settled in Tasmania after the death of his father. His mother married a second time, to Maurice O'Connor. She died in Ireland in April 1927. Caroline's daughter Harriet Monica (known as Monica) married Maurice Gruggen in 1883. They lived in Moosomin, Saskatchewan, Canada. As far as is known, they had no children.

SELECT BIBLIOGRAPHY

Works by Caroline Chisholm

Female Immigration, Considered, in a Brief Account of the Sydney Immigrants' Home, James Tegg, Sydney, 1842.

Prospectus of a Work to be Entitled 'Voluntary Information from the People of New South Wales' Respecting the Social Conditions of the Middle and Working Classes in that Colony, W. A. Duncan, Sydney, 1845.

Emigration and Transportation Relatively Considered, in a Letter Dedicated by Permission to Earl Grey by Mrs Chisholm with Voluntary Statements, Nos. 1 to 19, John Ollivier, London, 1847.

Comfort for the Poor! Meat Three Times a Day!!! Voluntary Information from the People of New South Wales Collected in that Colony in 1845–46, London, 1849.

The A.B.C. of Colonization. In a Series of Letters by Mrs Chisholm, No. 1 Addressed to the Gentlemen Forming the Committee of the Family Colonization Loan Society, viz. Lord Ashley, M.P., the Right Hon. Sydney Herbert M.P., the Hon. Vernon Smith, M.P., John Tidd Pratt, F. G. P. Neison, Esq., M. Monsell, Esq., M.P., having Appended A Letter to Lord Ashley, and the Rules of the Family Colonization Loan Society, John Ollivier, London, 1850.

Mrs Chisholm's Advice to Emigrants, reprinted from the *Liverpool Mercury*, Liverpool, 1853; printed by T. Brakell, Cook Street.

Little Joe, first published in the *Empire*, 26 December 1859 to 15 May 1860, reprinted in one volume by John Moran, Preferential Publications, Ashgrove, Australia, 1991.

Four Political Lectures by Caroline Chisholm, published by John Moran as *Radical in Bonnet and Shawl*, Preferential Publications, Ashgrove, Australia, 1994.

Biographies

Anstruther, G. Elliot, *Caroline Chisholm, The Emigrants' Friend*, Catholic Truth Society, London, 1916.

Bogle, Joanna, *Caroline Chisholm: The Emigrant's Friend*, Gracewing, Fowler Wright Books, Herefordshire, England, 1993.

Hoban, Mary, *Caroline Chisholm – A Biography Fifty-One Pieces of Wedding Cake*, Polding Press, Melbourne, 1984, first published under the title: *Fifty-One Pieces of Wedding Cake*, Jim Lowden Printing, Kilmore, 3601, in 1973.

Kiddle, Margaret, *Caroline Chisholm*, Melbourne University Press, 1957 (first published 1950). Abridged edition, 1969. Reprinted with Introduction by Patricia Grimshaw, 1990.

Mackenzie, Eneas, *Memoirs of Mrs Caroline Chisholm, with an Account of her Philanthropic Labours, in India, Australia & England. To which is added A History of the Family Colonization Loan Society with its Rules, Regulations, and Pledges. Also the Question Answered who Ought to Emigrate*, Webb, Millington & Co, London, 1852.

—— *The Emigrant's Guide to Australia with Memoir of Mrs Chisholm*, Clarke, Beeton & Co, London, 1853.

Stinson, Rodney, *Unfeigned Love – Historical Accounts of Caroline Chisholm and her Work*, Yorkcross Pty Ltd, Sydney, 2008.

Sutherland, Wendy, *Great Australians, Caroline Chisholm*, Melbourne Oxford University Press, 1967.

Swann, Margaret, *Caroline Chisholm, Friend to the Unemployed and Migrants, New South Wales and Victoria, 1838 to 1866*, Sydney, 1925.

Articles

Cohen, M. L., 'Caroline Chisholm and Jewish Immigration', in *Australian Jewish History Society*, v. 2. 1944.

Connole, Patrick, 'Caroline Chisholm: The Irish Chapter', in *Australia and Ireland 1788–1988 Bicentenary Essays*, ed. Colm Kiernan, Gill & Macmillan, Dublin, 1986.

Dark, Eleanor, 'Caroline Chisholm and her Times', in Eldershaw, Flora, *The Peaceful Army – A Memorial to the Pioneer Women of Australia 1788 to 1938*, Women's Advisory Council, Sydney, 1938; reprinted Penguin Books Australia Ltd, 1988.

Harris, B., *What has Mrs Caroline Chisholm done for the Colony of New South Wales?*, James Cole, Sydney, 1862.

Hoban, Mary, 'New Light on the Caroline Chisholm Story', in *Footprints*, Vol. 3. No. 2, October, 1977.

Kiddle, Margaret, 'Caroline Chisholm in New South Wales, 1838–46', in *Australia and New Zealand Historical Studies*, April 1942–November 1943.

Kingston, Beverley, 'Caroline Chisholm Revisited', in *The Australian Catholic Record*, Vol. LIV, No. 4, October 1977.

Luscombe, T. R., 'Caroline Chisholm – Keeper of the National Conscience', in *Builders and Crusaders*, 1967.

Mitchelet, Jules, *La Femme*, Oeuvres Completes, Paris, 1862 (translation).

Murtagh, James G., *Caroline Chisholm, who was she ? Was she a Saint ?*, Catholic Radio and Television Committee, Australia, 1966.

Pearson, Edith, *Ideals and Realities – Essays*, R. T. Washbourne Ltd, London, 1914.

Swann, Margaret, 'Caroline Chisholm', *Journal of the Royal Australian Historical Society*, Vol. vi, Part 2, 1920.

Walker, Carole, Littlewood, Jane L., 'A Second Moses in Bonnet and Shawl: Caroline Chisholm, 1808–1877', in *Recusant History – A Journal of Research in Post-Reformation Catholic History in the British Isles*, May 1995, Vol. 22, No. 3.

Walker, Carole, 'Setting the Record Straight: Caroline Chisholm née Jones, 1808–1877, The Early Years – Northampton', in *Northamptonshire Past and Present', The Journal of the Northamptonshire Record Society*, Number 56, 2003.

APPENDIX 1

The will of William Jones

I William Jones of the Town of Northampton in the County of Northampton Hog Jobber being of sound and disposing mind memory and understanding, praised be God for the same, Do make and ordain this my last will and Testament in manner and form following that is to say I give and devise unto my Son Robert Jones his heirs and assigns for ever All that my Close or inclosed ground with the appurtenances situate and being near Castle Hills within the liberties of the said Town of Northampton now in my own occupation and which I purchased of John Clarke. I give and devise unto my Daughter Caroline Jones her heirs and assigns for ever All that my messuage or tenement with the appurtenances situate standing and being in Bearward Street in the said Town of Northampton now or late in the tenure or occupation of my Son William Jones. I give and bequeath unto my dear wife Sarah Jones the sum of five hundred pounds of lawful money of Great Britain to be paid to her immediately after my decease. I give and bequeath unto my son James Jones and my Daughter Elizabeth Pettit the Sum of £100 pounds a piece of lawful money of Great Britain to be paid at the end of six Calendar months next after my decease. I give and forgive unto my Sons William Jones and George Jones and my daughter Mary Smith all monies by me advanced to or for them respectively. I give and devise unto my said wife and her assigns during her life all that my appurtenances to the same belonging situate and being in the Mayorhold in the said Town of Northampton now in my own possession and occupation and from and after the decease of my said wife and subject wheresaid estate for life therein I give and devise the said last mentioned premises unto and equally between my five children by my said wife, namely Charlotte, Thomas, Mary Ann, Sarah and Harriet their heirs and assigns for ever as tenants in Common and not as joint tenants and in case any or either of my said five Children give and devise the share or shares of him her or them so dying unto the Survivors or Survivor of them his her and their heirs and assigns for ever with like benefit of survivorship. As to all the real residue and remainder of my goods chattels effects ready money securities for money and personal estate whatsoever and wheresoever after and subject to the payment of my debts the aforesaid legacies and my funeral expenses I give and bequeath the same and every part thereof unto my said wife and my brother Plowman Jones upon Trust to put and place the same out at interest on such security or securities permit my said wife to receive the interest and annual produce thereof for her life for the better support and maintenance of herself and her said Children and from and after the decease of my said wife upon trust to pay and divide all the said residue and remainder of my said personal estate unto and equally between my said five last mentioned children share and share alike and I make constitute and appoint my said wife and my said Brother Plowman Jones Executrix and Executor of this my last Will and Testament and also Guardians to such of my said Children as shall be under the age of twenty-one years at the time of my decease during their respective minority. Provided always and my mind and will is that it shall and may be lawful to and for my said wife and my said Brother (if they shall think proper) or the survivor of them to pay and advance any sum or sums of money for the putting and placing and apprentice or otherwise advancing any or either of my said five children in the world as they shall think fit so as the sum to be advance for any one child do not exceed such particular childs share of the said residue of my personal estate and lastly I do hereby revoke and make void all former and all other wills by me at any time herefore made. In witness whereof I have to this my last will and testament contained in this and the previous sheet of paper set my hand and that to wish my hand to the preceding sheet and my hand and seal to the second or last sheet the 4th day of April in the year of our Lord Christ 1814.

The mark of William Jones

Witnessed:
Rob Abbey
Geo Abbey
Wm. Penfold (sic)

The 1824 Pigot's directory lists under Attorneys Robt. Abbey & Son of Gold Street. The 1830 directory lists under Attorneys George Abbey of Gold Street. George Abbey was by that time Coroner for Northamptonshire and the Secretary of the Law Society in the County. The signature of the third witness is difficult to decipher. It could be William Penfold, and may have been that of a clerk.

Sarah and Harriett their heirs and assigns for ever as tenants in Comm
as joint tenants And in Case any or either of my said five Children s
to die without issue under the age of twenty one Years then I give and de
or shares of him her or them so dying unto the Survivors or Survivor of
and their heirs and assigns with like benefit of Survivorship. As to all t
and remainder of my goods chattels effects ready money securities for mon
estate whatsoever and wheresoever after and subject to the payment of
aforesaid legacies and my funeral Expences I give and bequeath the sa
[illegible] thereof unto my said wife and my brother Plowman Jones upon
and place the same out at interest on such Security or Securities as they
of them shall think proper and pay to or permit my said wife to
interest and annual produce thereof for her life for the better support
of herself and her said Children And from and after the decease of
upon trust to pay and divide all the said residue and remainder of
personal Estate unto and equally between my said five last mentioned
and share alike And I nominate constitute and appoint my said wife
said Brother Plowman Jones Executrix and Executor of this my la
Testament and also Guardians to such of my said Children as shall
age of twenty one Years at the time of my decease during their respec
Provided always and my mind and will is that it shall and ma
to and for my said wife and my said Brother if they shall think fi

The Mark of
William Jones

Witnesses
[illegible]
[illegible]
[illegible]

Courtesy of Northampton Record Office

APPENDIX 2

Descendants of Archibald and Caroline Chisholm

* died in infancy

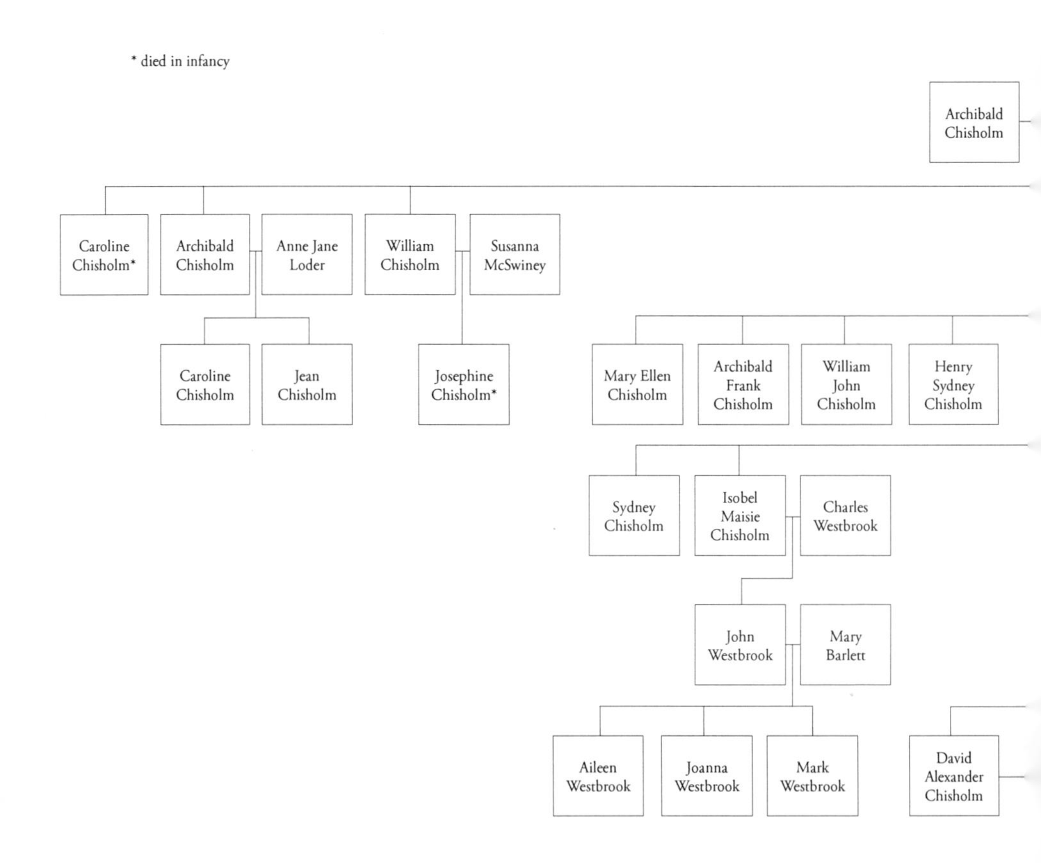

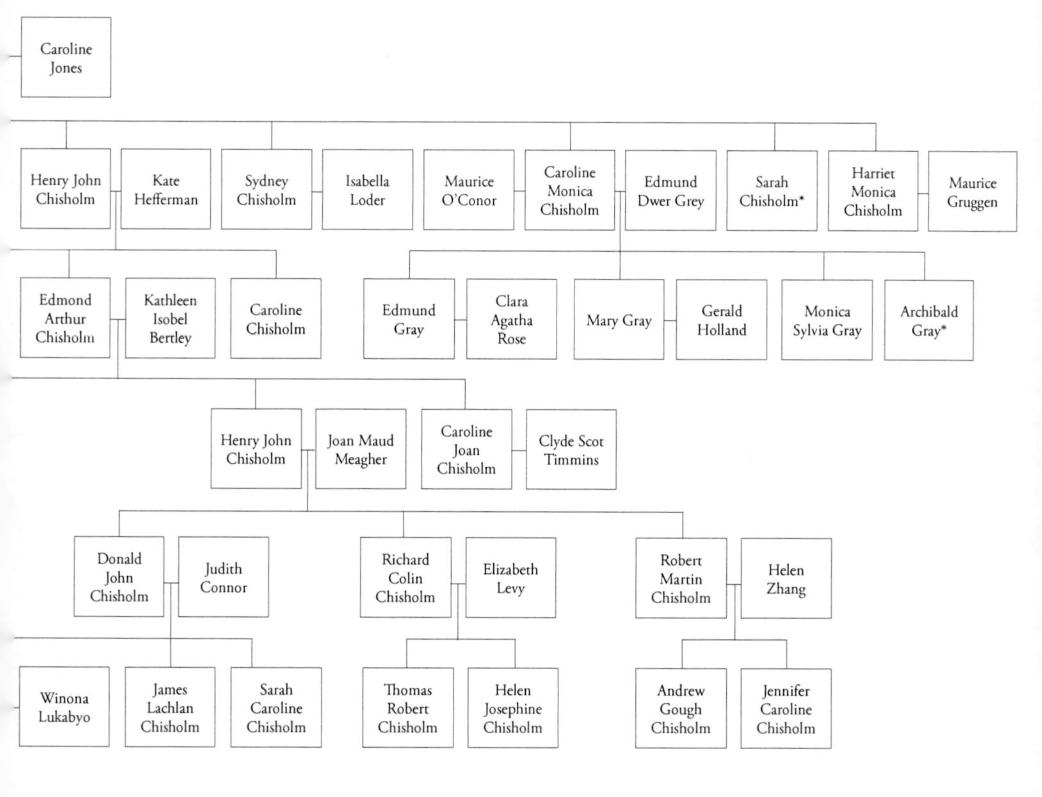

Caroline Jones
Henry John Chisholm
Kate Hefferman
Sydney Chisholm
Isabella Loder
Maurice O'Conor
Caroline Monica Chisholm
Edmund Dwer Grey
Sarah Chisholm*
Harriet Monica Chisholm
Maurice Gruggen
Edmond Arthur Chisholm
Kathleen Isobel Bertley
Caroline Chisholm
Edmund Gray
Clara Agatha Rose
Mary Gray
Gerald Holland
Monica Sylvia Gray
Archibald Gray*
Henry John Chisholm
Joan Maud Meagher
Caroline Joan Chisholm
Clyde Scot Timmins
Donald John Chisholm
Judith Connor
Richard Colin Chisholm
Elizabeth Levy
Robert Martin Chisholm
Helen Zhang
Winona Lukabyo
James Lachlan Chisholm
Sarah Caroline Chisholm
Thomas Robert Chisholm
Helen Josephine Chisholm
Andrew Gough Chisholm
Jennifer Caroline Chisholm

Family tree of William Jones and Sarah Jones *(née Allum)*

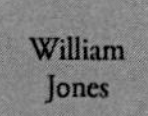

NOTE: This family tree is sectioned into 3 parts.
1 is left, 2 is middle, and 3 is right.

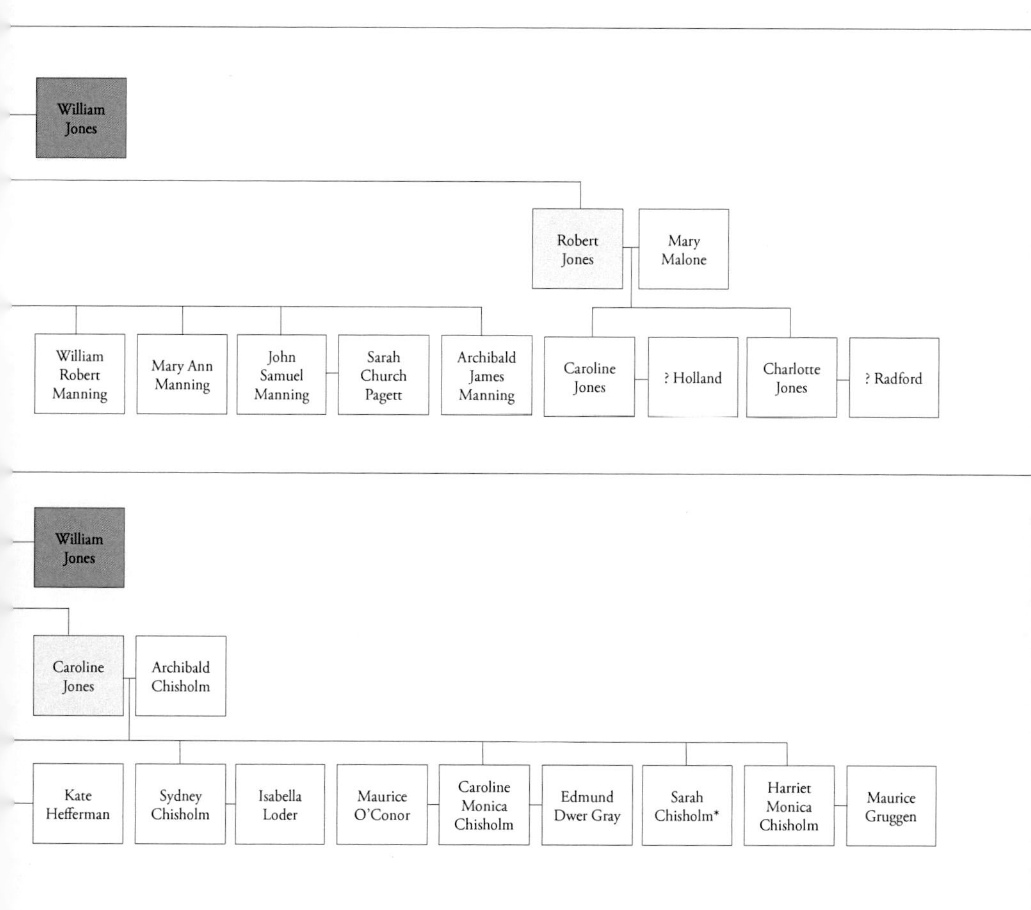

Family tree of Archibald Chisholm

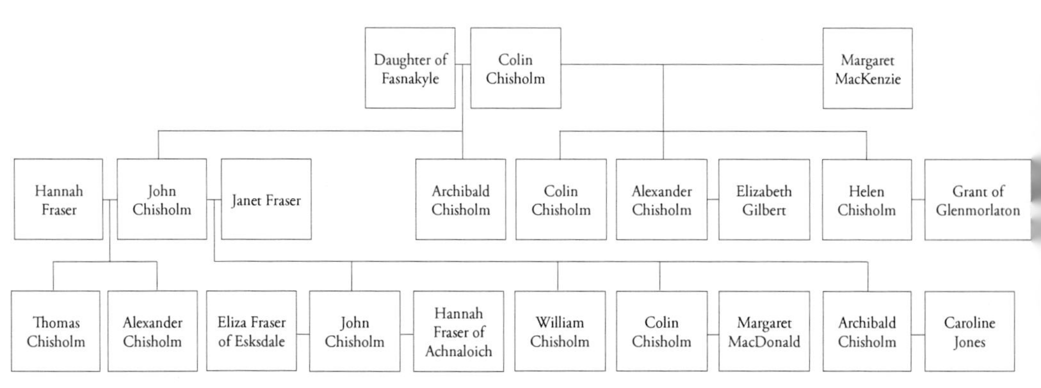

APPENDIX 3

Phrenological examination

Mr James De Ville made the following observations after subjecting Caroline Chishom to a phrenological examination.

Brighton 29th July 1833.

> This Lady's memory is rather extraordinary. There are very few persons who possess so strong an one. Few people have greater power in the acquirement of languages. If she have attempted improvisation she would have excelled in it:– there are few organisations with more power for it. Has a very high sense of justice, but she must take care of it. If offended her expressions will be strong.
>
> Attachments and friendships few, and very strong. Diffident among strangers, but cheerful in Society. It is not often a Lady takes to Mathematics, but this individual would not find it difficult. If she could take up poetry she would do well at it. With Theology and Sacred History she should be well acquainted. Has a high sense of Religion.

This organisation is not confined to a single thing:- it would give power in many, though to afford her pleasure it must partake of the practical feeling. Theology must have undergone a good deal of consideration. Has a severe struggle with herself and inward feelings. Annoys herself more than her neighbours. Knows herself better than others. There are few organisations so good if it have been well cultivated. Drawing is not difficult. Music pleasing. This organisation partakes more of the male than the female character. Is capable of going through a great deal of struggling with difficulties. Fond of approbations, but does not stoop to servile means to obtain it: will have a little struggle with this organ: Kind and benevolent as far as her means go:- Love of children strongly developed.

This is the most powerful organisation which I have seen in Brighton, with one exception (Mrs M.). This is amazingly powerful, more destined by nature for a Male than a Female head. It is a most general organisation, and though it may now be confined to one subject it can apply and excel in any. Mathematics, Natural History, The Sciences, Chemistry, Analysis etc. She could excel in anything. This organisation is most like Certina, an Italian Improvisation, and was originally intended for a Male! Her memory is so strong, she can excel in anything and would never be confined to one subject. If she were to apply to the dead languages she would become a proficient. There is nothing she would take up in which she could not excel. Form and size are good. Miniature and landscape painting, and drawing generally could be acquired with facility on this account. Few would go more readily into the Hindostanee language:- having memory to recollect the characters. She has a very strong memory. Music (organ of) requires more development, has enough power in Time (organ of).

She principally wants a quicker arrangement of her ideas:– she has the power good, but a little more would make it gigantic. It is not in proportion to the rest of the organisation. She will excel in the Arts and Sciences. There are not half a dozen male organisations in the Kingdom with such a powerful memory. She is a thorough improvisatrice–give her the subject, and she will make you a speech on it; or write sheets full.

She is communicative on common topics, but has judgement to discriminate when she may speak and when be silent; would not disclose a matter of importance—would suffer death first, rather than do so:- did the honour or character of another depend upon it. Has a gigantic organisation, more powerful than that of the Marquis Mascati.

Signed James De Ville
Brighton Jan 30th 1833

There follows a list of the measurements of Caroline Chisholm's head. Also written across the paper at the bottom are the words 'For Henry'. Presumably the papers were divided amongst the family and this Report was for Henry Chisholm, Caroline's son.

Phrenology is basically the study of the shape and bumps of the skull. It was based on the theory of the Austrian Physician Franz Josef Gall who believed that such features revealed measurable psychological and intellectual traits. James De Ville (1777–1846), rising from humble beginnings to a journeyman moulder in plaster, and seller of plaster figures, went on to become a prominent participant in the field of phrenology. He started his career with little knowledge of the subject, but attended lectures and went on to collect casts as records of facts in evidence of phrenology. He had a collection of some 2,050 casts or skulls of men of every grade in society. Many of the casts were made without cost to the sitter. De Ville invented a new method of moulding from the living head to avoid inconvenience to his sitters. As there is an apparent discrepancy in the dates of the examination at the top and bottom of the page, this could well be because De Ville did the examination in January, but the report was not written up until July. De Ville received little education and his handwriting and vocabulary were notorious. The report could have been written up for him at a later date. (Detail from *The Phrenological Journal*, vol. 6, 1830; vol. 14, 1841; vol. 19, 1846).

The above is a transcription of the Examination that is held at the Mitchell Library, State Library of New South Wales (Miscellaneous Papers re Caroline Chisholm, c.1833–1854 32 CY2097-SAC19/1-2 ML AC 19-A/1-10). The report was also included in Mackenzie's *Memoirs* (pp. 144–148). It is curious to note that Mackenzie wrote a book on Phrenology, titled *Phrenology Explained and Exemplified*, published by R. Hardwicke, c.1855. It is interesting to speculate that his interest in the subject followed the writing of his *Memoirs* of Caroline (1852) and the inclusion of the phrenological examination. Mackenzie writes of the report:

> Unknown to De Ville, she [Caroline] was urged to present herself to him, and not enter into conversation, when that celebrated manipulator thus declares his opinion of the organisation that appeared to him.

Following this, Mackenzie writes:

This professor of Phrenology remarked, on presenting the above document, 'I am willing to stake the truth of Phrenological science on the development of this head being in accordance with the mind and actions of the individual'. Those who have had the honour of intimately knowing Mrs Chisholm, and others who have read of her acts may form a judgment of the reliance to be placed in Phrenological science from the above curious document, given before she attained the public position she now occupies.

APPENDIX 4

Chronology of Caroline Chisholm's lectures and meetings in England

Date	Place and purpose of meeting
14. 4.1850	Group Meeting at 3 Charlton Crescent, Islington. Attended by The Rt. Hon. Sidney Herbert, M.P.
4. 5.1850	Preliminary Meeting, *FCLS*, 3 Charlton Crescent, Islington. 200 people attended.
1. 6.1850	Group Meeting *FCLS*, 3 Charlton Crescent, Islington.
16. 7.1850	Emigration Meeting, Royal British Institution, City Road, London.
28. 9.1850	Departure of the *Slains Castle*, first ship of *FCLS*.
29. 4.1851	Chisholm led a party of emigrants about to depart on the ship *Blundell* on a visit to the Great Exhibition, Crystal Palace, London.
2. 5.1851	Farewell Meeting on board the *Blundell* before the ship sailed from Gravesend on 4.5.1851.

22.9.1851	East India Docks, meeting aboard the *Athenian* before it set sail.
18.2.1852	Emigration Meeting, British Institution, Tabernacle Row, City Road, London.
7. 4.1852	Emigration Meeting, Provident Institute, 49 Ann Street, Birmingham.
17.5.1852	Emigration Meeting, Imperial Hotel, Cork, Ireland.
22.5.1852	Chisholm attended convent of the Sisters of Mercy, Baggot Street, Dublin, followed by visit to Hospital of the Sisters of Charity, St Stephen's Green, Dublin. (This was Chisholm's first visit to Ireland–she spent 47 hours steaming from Liverpool to Cork, then travelled Cork to Dublin by railway. Dublin to Kingstown on board the *Prince Arthur* to Holyhead.
30. 6.1852	Emigration Meeting, Domestic Mission House, Spicer Street, Spitalfields, London.
27.7.1852	Group Meeting, Family Colonisation, British Institution, Cowper Street, City Road.
18. 8.1852	Farewell Meeting of passengers sailing on the *Ballangeich* from Southampton.
23.8.1852	Group Meeting—Family Colonisation—Parochial School Rooms, Clapham.
13. 9.1852	Farewell and Emigration Meeting, Queenstown, Cork, before emigrants left on *Peru*.

13. 9.1852	Town Hall, Southampton. Emigration meeting Chaired by Samuel Sidney suggesting Southampton as an emigration port in favour of Caroline's plan of emigration.
30. 9.1852	Launch of ship *W. S. Lindsay*, Newcastle.
9.1852	Two free lectures given by Samuel Sidney during the early part of November on Mrs Chisholm's behalf at the Domestic Mission, Essex Street Chapel, London.
2.10.1852	Group Meeting held in Lecture Room, Newcastle.
4.10.1852	Emigration Meeting, Parochial School, Clapham Common, London.
10.1852	Mrs Chisholm held a very crowded meeting at the Essex Street Chapel, Domestic Mission, London, with a view to give information to clerks and governesses intending to emigrate to Australia.
3. 1.1853	Emigration Meeting, Mechanics Institute, Greenwich, London.
26. 1.1853	Emigration Meeting, Mechanics Institute, Greenwich, London.
25/26.2.1853	Two Emigration Meetings, Lecture Room, Mechanics Institute, Northampton.
26/27.2.1853	Emigration Meetings held in the Music Room, Corn Exchange, Northampton.
3.1853	Local Intelligence, Emigration Meeting, Town Hall, Brighton, Sussex.

9. 4.1853	Emigration Meeting, Lecture Hall, Fair Street, Horselydown (Horsleydown) London, at the request of the Committee of the Bermondsey and Horsleydown Mutual Improvement Association.
15. 4.1853	Glasgow. Meetings to be held in the Town. Caroline was in Glasgow to look at ship(s) being built on the Clyde to her specifications.
21. 4.1853	Emigration Meeting, Mechanics Institute, Liverpool.
23. 4.1853	Emigration Meeting, Concert Hall, Lord Nelson Street, Liverpool.
c.26.4.1853	Meetings to be held in Glasgow to look at ship(s) being built on the Clyde to Chisholm's specifications.
30.5.1853	Address at the Guildhall, Bristol of Family Colonisation Society.
8. 7.1853	Chisholm arrived in Rome to collect William from the Propaganda College.
9.8.1853	Public Meeting, London Tavern, Bishopgate Street, 12 noon for 1 o'clock to raise 'Testimonial to Mrs Chisholm'. Mr Vernon Smith in the Chair.
10.1853	Social tea meeting to discuss emigration, Domestic Mission, Spicer Street, Spitalfields, London.
10. 4.1854	Farewell meeting for Chisholm's departure on *Ballarat*, attended by Samuel Sidney and Douglas Jerrold, London.

The above is to give an indication of Caroline's meetings and lectures held in Britain following the foundation of the *FCLS* in 1849, and prior to her return to Australia in 1854. Caroline also toured the continent, arriving in Rome in July 1853. Presumably this was at the end of her tour for she collected William from the Propaganda College in Rome. Ill health had made it impossible for William to continue his studies as a Priest. (Dates obtained from various newspaper cuttings and Annual Reports of the Domestic Mission.)

Hoban suggests that there is evidence that Caroline also spoke at a *Christian Emigration* gathering, at a meeting of the *Postal Reform Association* and that she was seated on the platform at an Anti-Slavery Meeting. At a lecture in Brighton, the economist Ricardo presided. Exact dates are not known.[1] Meetings were held prior to the sailing of most of the *FCLS* ships. Not all have been detailed.

Remarkably during this period Caroline gave birth to three daughters, two of whom survived. Caroline Monica was born on 13 May 1848; Sarah was born in January 1850 but died in August that year. Harriet Monica was born on 24 July 1851. Sidney was born on board ship on 6 August 1846 just prior to the Chisholms arrival in Britain. The other surviving sons were born in 1836, 1837 and 1839.

APPENDIX 5

The Female School of Industry for the Daughters of European Soldiers

The chief object of this Institution is to enable such European Soldiers as may feel disposed to remove their children from the Barracks and Putchery Lines. A House for the reception is to be procured in Black Town, Madras, where the children will be instructed in reading, writing, arithmetic, needlework, and domestic management. Their religious instruction and moral conduct will be made an object of particular attention.

Rules

1. Each child is to come provided with two plates, one cup and saucer, one knife and fork, one table and teaspoon, one drinking mug, and one common box for clothes.
2. Each child is to be furnished with a separate bed; they are to be clothed in one uniform dress (after they have worn out such clothes as they may have brought with them to school) and to have one general mess.

3. They are to get up at an hour so as to be able to take some recreation in the cool of the morning, either on the Beach or Esplanade, they are first however (after having washed themselves) to say a short prayer, and after they have come in to say their regular morning prayers, and then to have their breakfast. The children are to be assembled for prayers and meals by the ringing of a bell. They are never to go out without being accompanied by either the mistress or matron of the school.
4. No child is to be sent or allowed to go to the Bazaar without the sanction of one of the managers.
5. A child can at any time be withdrawn from the school, but will not afterwards be re-admitted to the establishment.
6. Parents who may have a daughter in this establishment may, during illness, send any of their younger children, on paying the expenses of their food.
7. Infant children will also be received from the Regiment Hospital a few hours daily, as the main object of this school is to teach girls the domestic duties according to the station in life they may expect to move in.

Offences	**Punishments**
For telling an untruth	To forfeit five tickets, and to be kept for that day separate from the other children in the school room that visitors may at once know the offender

For stealing, and however trifling offence	The same punishment as above
Second offence	Black bracelets in addition
In breaking crockery, if immediately acknowledged	No punishment
but if discovered afterwards by the mistress or matron	To forfeit three tickets
Parties to concealment	To forfeit one ticket; for conniving at trifles may in time lead to great crimes
If discovered quarrelling or fighting	To be put on low diet for a day, the same punishment for all concerned
If sulky for six hours or a day	Low diet double the time
Any girl who refuses to assist in making a pudding	Not to partake of the same
If any part of the dress is torn at play	The girl to be immediately sent into a room to repair it

A black book is to be kept, into which all offences and punishments are to be entered by the mistress, the offenders are to be made to affix their names thereto. This book to be shown to every visiting member.

Address to be Read by the Mistress

My dear little Girls—It is my wish that you should have read to you once a month the list of punishments. The rod in appearance is quite frightful, and I think you have the same opinion of it, and I trust you will look upon the Bracelets with a determination never to wear them. It is, I assure you, much easier to be good than to be bad, and you must be the one or the other. It will be a very shocking thing and would distress your parents and friends to see your name in the Black Book. If you tell lies, I fear you will soon learn to steal, for one generally follows the other; and if you steal sugar and little things, I fear you will in time steal broaches, and I dread to think what your end may be. But I hope better things of you, and fully expect you will pay great attention to the good instructions you receive, and be really good girls. But if you are idle you cannot be good. I therefore hope you will be industrious, this will be setting a good example to the natives, for let me tell you, and I speak the truth, that there is no situation in life in which you cannot do some good. I wish you never to forget how kind your parents are to place you in a situation where you are not surrounded by vice and wickedness. They are now giving up some of their comforts to add to yours, and it is not enough that you love them and feel grateful, but you must show your gratitude by your good conduct, and learn to be useful now, that you may hereafter be of real use to them, and perhaps in their old age; think if your mother should be ill, how happy it would make you to be able to nurse her and make her nice jellies, and light puddings, and do all that was required for her. You cannot, my children, think how dearly a mother loves, and the comfort she would feel in having a daughter for a nurse, and you must learn to do those things before you can have this pleasure, and you have now the opportunity. Think too how rejoiced your father would be to see you do all this, and how much such conduct would repay him for having given up his Arrack allowance to make you a good and dutiful girl. I wish you also to consider how proud your parents will be of you, I fancy I already hear your father say, in honest pride, that my girl can keep accounts, cook a dinner, and she is only fourteen years of age; and your mother says, yes, and make a shirt and cut it out as well if not better than I can. That you will be able to do these things I fully expect, and I have no doubt but you will have a great pleasure in doing so, and your being able to do them will give you a proper feeling of pride and independence, that is, if your parents should die, you would be able by your good conduct and management to support yourselves and little brothers and sisters, for God will never forsake the good. Before I conclude this, I must again refer to that frightful Rod, that shocking Black Book, and those ugly Bracelets, and as I think you will, with pride becoming soldier's daughters, consider it a disgrace that they should be seen. I will promise you, that if at the end of one year the Rod has never been used, that you shall have a day's holiday to bury or burn it, and that you shall invite your parents to be present on the occasion, giving them cake etc. made by your own hands. When the Rod is fairly out of the house, the Rewards will be distributed, and the ladies and gentlemen who have so kindly supported this institution shall be invited to attend at the distribution of the prizes, and you will know how necessary it is that the Rod should be removed ere this could take place. Your united good conduct could also remove the Bracelets and Black Book. Try then, my dear little girls, to be good, never tell lies, never steal the smallest thing, never fight and quarrel, and never make use of bad words, and obey and do what you are told, and you will then be the pride of your parents, a credit to your religion, and the admiration of all your friends.

To the Matron and Mistress

You must never forget that children are early lovers of justice, and that peace and harmony cannot dwell where favouritism reigns. In this establishment, much will depend upon your conduct, as children learn more from example than precept. They are generally close and faithful imitators of those they reside with, and will judge by your acts and not by your professions; they will in the twinkling of an eye discover whether the way to your favour is the high *road of sincerity* or by the path of *hypocrisy and dissimulation* and will either love and respect you, or fear and *despise* you. If you rule justly, you will find it easy to govern; encourage them to be kind to each other, and lovers of peace; reprove them for their faults privately, and if possible without the knowledge of each other; never bring up old faults; be just and impartial in the distribution of tickets; and enter faithfully into the Black Book all punishments and the cause of them; and if you should have any *particular* complaint against any one of the children, report the same to the Managers that they may direct you how to act. You are not to use the Rod except you have permission of the visiting Manager. It will however be better that the children should not be aware that it is necessary for you to obtain this permission.

Extracts from the Assistant Housekeepers' Account Book:

- Breakfast ready at half-past seven.
- Weighed the bread and meat, found them correct.
- Gave out the stores, 3 measures of rice, quarter pound tea, 1lb. Sugar.
- Extra, 2 spoonfuls of barley to make barley water for Mary Macmillin, who is not very well.
- There are only 20 measures of rice remaining in stores.
- For dinner, boiled mutton, curry and rice. Remarks: rice too much boiled.
- At two o'clock, made Mary Macmillin a cup of Tea. She is now much better.
- As there was some cold meat left, and a small quantity of rice which would not keep until tomorrow, we made it into pish-pash and gave it to the poor blind woman.
- The tea leaves were given to the other poor women as usual.
- The tea kettle wants repairing.
- Paid the butcher's bill, 4r. la 6d.

Dated June 1st 1836.

Signed by the Assistant House-keepers: Mary Smith, 13 years; Jane White, 12 years; Kitty McCarthy, 8 years

Questions to be answered by Mary Smith, Jane White, Kitty McCarthy:

- How long was the rice boiling?
- By referring to the accounts, I find there ought to be five pounds of sugar in stores, how do you account for the deficiency?
- What have you done with the butcher's receipt?
- What use did you make of the boiled barley after draining of the water?

NOTES

Introduction

1 E. Windschuttle, ed., *Women, Class and History: Feminist Perspectives on Australia 1788–1978*, Fontana/Collins, 1980, pp. 53, 54.

2 *Ibid.*

3 Caroline Chisholm to Earl Grey, 25 January 1847.

4 *The Argus*, 13 June 1857.

5 Caroline Chisholm, Report of Sydney's Immigrants' Home, 1842.

6 Mary Hoban, *Caroline Chisholm – A Biography, Fifty-One Pieces of Wedding Cake*, Polding Press, Melbourne, 1984, p. x. First published under the title *Fifty-One Pieces of Wedding Cake*, Jim Lowden Printing, Kilmore, 1973.

7 Joanna Bogle, *Caroline Chisholm – The Emigrant's Friend*, Gracewing, Fowler Wright Books, Herefordshire, England, 1993, pp. viii, 155.

The Early Years, 1808–1832

1 Jane Rendall, *Women in an Industrializing Society: England 1750–1880*, Basil Blackwell Ltd, Oxford, 1990, pp. 38, 40.

2 Dorothy A. Rice, *Wootton – An Ordinary Village*, privately published by Dorothy Rice, 1991, p. 20.

3 The 1777 Duston Militia list notes that William Jones, Shoemaker, was exempt from serving as he had young children.

4 *Pigot's Trade Directory*, 1824.

5. NRO, Northampton Wills, William Jones, 1814. St Sepulchre's Poor Law Books.
6. *Pigot's Trade Directory*, 1824.
7. Caroline Chisholm, *Little Joe*; first published in the *Empire*, 26 December 1859 to 15 May 1860; reprinted in one volume by John Moran, Preferential Publications, Ashgrove, Australia, 1991, p. 74.
8. Edith Pearson, *Ideals and Realities – Essays*, R. T. Washbourne Ltd, London, 1914, p. 71.
9. Eneas Mackenzie, *Memoirs of Mrs Caroline Chisholm, with an account of her Philanthropic Labours, in India, Australia & England. To which is added A History of the Family Colonization Loan Society with its Rules, Regulations, and Pledges. Also the Question answered who ought to emigrate.* Webb, Millington & Co, London, 1852, p. 2 (hereinafter called '*Memoirs*').
10. Pearson, 1914, p. 73.
11. *Caroline Chisholm*, Melbourne University Press, 1957, p. 3. First published 1950. Abridged edition, 1969; reprinted with Introduction by Patricia Grimshaw, 1990.
12. Caroline Chisholm, *Little Joe*, first published in The Empire, 26 December 1859 to 15 May 1860; reprinted in one volume by John Moran, Preferential Publications, Ashgrove, Australia, 1991, p. 19.
13. *Ibid.*
14. Wages varied, as did the variety of jobs, during the later part of the eighteenth and early part of the nineteenth centuries. Britain had almost continuously been at war with France from 1793 to 1815 and this had an effect on the economy of the country, especially with Napoleon's blockade of England designed to bring the 'nation of shopkeepers' to their knees by preventing them from selling their goods overseas. The wages of farm workers in Sussex were roughly 9 shillings a week (45 pence in current money) in 1790, rising slowly to 13s. (65 pence) a week in 1810. Handloom weavers in Bolton, who in the early years of the nineteenth century went around with £5 notes stuck in their hats, saw their wages drop from 25s. (£1.25p) to 15s. (75 pence) a week between 1805 and 1808. C. P. Hill, *British Economic and Social History 1700–1964*, Edward Arnold (Publishers) Ltd, 1970 (third edition.)
15. Moran, 1991, p. 8.
16. Samuel Sidney's *Emigrant's Journal*, August 1849, p. 269.
17. Pearson, 1914, p. 92.
18. *Pigot's Trade Directory*, 1824.
19. Reverend W. J. Bain, *A Paper on the Early History of Sunday Schools especially in Northamptonshire with appendix.* Taylor and Sons, Northampton, 1875, Appendix I.
20. Moran, 1991, p. 3.

21 Caroline Chisholm, *op cit.*

22 Eneas Mackenzie, *The Emigrant's Guide to Australia with Memoir of Mrs Chisholm*, Clarke, Beeton & Co, London, 1853, p. 5 (hereinafter called *Emigrant's Guide*).

23 R. L. Greenhall, *A History of Northamptonshire and the soke of Peterborough*, Phillimore, Chichester, West Sussex, 2000, pp. 101, 115.

24 Michael Brock, *The Great Reform Act*, Hutchinson University Library, London, 1973.

25 A study of Caroline's family indicates that Caroline's half-brother George had a son Joseph, baptised at St Sepulchre's on 11 April 1815. George Jones and his family lived in Bearward Street, off the Mayorhold, Northampton. Joseph would have been fifteen when Caroline married Archibald in December 1830. Joseph Jones of Bearward Street, Northampton, signed as Secretary, on behalf of the Committee, an eight-page pamphlet that was delivered to each of the Northampton shoe manufacturers in August 1838. The pamphlet was entitled 'An appeal from the Northampton Society of Operative Cordwainers, to the Boot and Shoe Manufacturers of Northampton, on behalf of the workman'. It had the subtitle 'Live, and let live'. Northampton Central Public Library, Boot and Shoe Collection, 3145.

26 Detail from Mr MacLeod, Genealogist, Highland Council, Inverness.

27 Catholic Directory, 1964, p. 45. II Scotland, A., The Vicars-Apostolic (1694–1878).

28 John Chisholm, Archibald's elder brother, born 16 August 1793 became a cadet in 1808. He was invalided out of the army in 1839, the year of his wife's death. Archibald's brother William joined the Company Army, the Madras Artillery. He was killed in action in 1818 at Corrygeum, Deccan, fighting against the Pelswah's army. Brother Colin was a solicitor in Inverness. Information acquired via the British Library India and Oriental Collections and with the kind help of Mr James MacRae of Inverness and his Chisholm family tree.

29 British Library India and Oriental Collection, 1/MILL/11/41, 375.

30 Mary Hoban, *Caroline Chisholm – A Biography - Fifty-One Pieces of Wedding Cake*, Polding Press, Melbourne, 1984, pp. 12–13; first published under the title: *Fifty-One Pieces of Wedding Cake*, Jim Lowden Printing, Kilmore, 3601, in 1973.

31 J. K. Stanford, *Ladies in the Sun – The Memsahibs' India 1790–1860*, The Galley Press, London, 1962, p. 65.

32 *Ibid.*

33 It was not until October 1836 that regimental Quartermasters were relieved from these duties, and the Officers of troops and companies made responsible for issuing the pay to the men. *History of the Madras Army*, v. 4, 1888, chapter XXVII, p. 461.

34 *Emigrant's Guide*, 1853, pp. 5, 6.

35 Janet Dunbar, *The Early Victorian Woman, Some Aspects of Her Life (1836–57)*, George G. Harrap & Co Ltd, London, Sydney, 1853, p. 20.

36 L. Davidoff & C. Hall, *Family Fortunes – Men and Women of the English Middle-Class 1780–1850*, Hutchinson, 1998, p. 323. First published 1987.

37 Kali Israel, *Name and Stories – Emilia Dilke and Victorian Culture*, New York, Oxford, Oxford University Press, 1999, p. 99.

38 George Eliot, *Middlemarch*, Penguin Books, Middx, 1965, p. 67; first published 1871–72.

39 Israel, *op cit.*, p. 99.

40 Both Charlotte and John Wright had had previous marriages. John had a daughter Frances who signed the marriage register.

41 John Gunning's sons followed in their father's footsteps and also served with the East India Company army.

42 Reverend James MacCaffrey, *History of the Catholic Church in the Nineteenth Century, 1789–1908*, M. H. Gill & Son Ltd, Dublin and Waterford, 1909. Vol. 2, p. 4.

43 W. D. Hussey, *British History 1815–1830*, Cambridge University Press, 1971, pp. 20–1.

44 Clifford Lines, *Companion to the Industrial Revolution, Facts on File*, New York, Oxford, Sydney, 1990, p. 94.

45 MacCaffrey, *op cit.*, p. 34.

46 William Cobbett, *Cobbett's England – A Selection from the Writings of William Cobbett*, edited by John Derry, Parkgate Books, London, 1997, pp. 109, 107.

47 James Dawson Burn, *The Autobiography of a Beggar Boy*, edited and introduced by David Vincent, London, Europa Publications Limited, 1978, p. 42; first published in 1855.

48 *Ibid.*, pp. 132, 133.

49 The sees of 1851 were Westminster, Beverley, Birmingham, Clifton, Hexham (later Hexham and Newcastle), Liverpool, Newport and Menevia, Northampton, Nottingham, Plymouth, Salford, Shrewsbury and Southwark. The title of Beverley disappeared in 1818 when the diocese was divided between the new sees of Leeds and Middlesbrough. David Mathew, *Catholicism in England – The Portrait of a Minority: Its Culture and Tradition*, Eyre & Spottiswoode, 1955, p. 199; first published in 1936.

50 E. R. Norman, *Anti-Catholicism in Victorian England*, George Allen & Unwin Ltd, 1968, p. 159.

51 J. W. Burrow, 'Faith, doubt and unbelief', *The Victorians – The Context of English Literature*, Laurence Lerner (ed.), Holmes and Meier Publishers, New York, 1978, p. 154.

52 Northampton Record Office, Northampton Wills, 1873.8.173. Will No. 73. Harriet Goode, née Jones died on 12 December 1872. Her will required her Trustees to sell

three properties, 112, 114 and 116 Great Russell Street, Northampton. The proceeds to be divided between niece Charlotte, the wife of Reverend John Broad, nephew John Manning of Rugby, Warwick, Cabinet Maker, and nephew Henry Chisholm, Melbourne, Australia. Later in the will Harriet's nieces Mrs Charlotte Radford and Mrs Caroline Holland, both residing at Brooklyn, New York, America, are mentioned. These are the daughters of Robert Jones, Caroline's brother who emigrated in 1821.

53 D. G. Paz, *Popular Anti-Catholicism in Mid-Victorian Britain*, Stanford University Press, 1992, p. 234 quoting *Northampton Herald*, 9 and 11 November 1850.

54 *Northampton Mercury*, 5 March 1853.

55 The *Northampton Herald*, 9 November 1850.

56 Paz, as above, p. 233.

57 E. J. Evans, *The Great Reform Act of 1832*, Methuen & Co Ltd, 1983, p. 26.

58 Eric Hopkins, *A Social History of the English Working Classes 1850–1945*, Edward Arnold, London, 1979, p. 33.

59 *Ibid.*, p. 33.

60 Caroline Chisholm, *Female Immigration, Considered, in a Brief Account of the Sydney Immigrants' Home*, James Tegg, Sydney, 1842, p. 77 (hereinafter called *Female Immigration*). The Bristol Riots, 29–31 October 1831. During the whole of Saturday, Bristol was in a state of considerable ferment from the arrival of Sir C. Wetherall, the Recorder. In the evening the multitude assembled before the Mansion House in Queen Square and smashed the windows in the front of the building with a volley of stones. The noise of the stones breaking the windows—a Bristol tune.

61 Victor A. Hatley, 'Some Aspects of Northampton's History, 1815–1851', *Northamptonshire Past and Present*, 1965/66, Vol. III, No. 6, pp. 243–9.

62 Evans, *op cit.*, pp. 36–7.

63 Caroline Chisholm, *Emigration and Transportation Relatively Considered, in a Letter dedicated by permission to Earl Grey by Mrs Chisholm with Voluntary Statements, Nos. 1 to 19*, John Ollivier, London, 1847, p. 3 (hereinafter called *Emigration & Transportation*).

India 1832–1838

1 On the passenger list were: Colonel McFane, H. M. 54 Regiment, Lieutenants, F. Chisholme [Archibald Chisholm], F. Carter and Mr M. Macintire and cadets Messrs. H. and G. Short. Madras Almanac 1883, British Library Oriental Department.

2 G. M. Young, *Early Victorian England 1830–1865*, two volumes, London, Oxford University Press, 1934, vol. 1, p, 392.

3 Inspection Report, 10 December 1837, British Library Oriental Department.

4 'Batta' was a hard-living allowance for discomfort and extra expense. Presumably when in the Presidency of Madras officers were able to obtain British supplies, i.e. beer, liquors, hams, cheese etc., at a cheaper rate than they would have done in the provinces.

5 British Library Oriental Department, *East India Register and Directory, 1839*, pp. vi and vii.

6 James De Ville (1777–1846) came from humble beginnings, and lacked the ability to write 'with clearness … and that in speaking he never could divest himself of certain phraseological peculiarities.' But he was respected for his work in the field of phrenology. He amassed a large collection of plaster casts and skulls. See 'A Memoir of the Late Mr James De Ville' by James P. Browne MD, *Phrenological Journal and Magazine of Moral Science*, London, 1846, pp. 329–44.

7 Previous biographies suggested that Caroline acted as a chaperone to several young ladies on the trip to India. But there was only one single young woman on board. Caroline may well have befriended her. The passengers accompanying Caroline were: Mrs Mathias, Mrs Harding and Miss Coffin, Captains Mathias and Scott; Lieutenants Harding and Tremlet, together with Mr Willy and two natives. Captain J. Short was again in charge of the *Elphinstone*.

8 J. K. Stanford, *Ladies in the Sun – The Memsahibs' India 1790–1860*, The Gallery Press, London, 1962, p. 36.

9 *Ibid.*

10 *Ibid.*, p. 64. Stanford uses the quotation from *A Six Years Diary* by James Slator Cumming, 9th Foot, Martin and Hood, 1847.

11 Anthony Sattin, *An Englishwoman in India – The Memoirs of Harriet Tytler 1828–1858*, Oxford University Press, 1986, p. xix.

12 Mackenzie, *Emigrants' Guide*, 1853, p. 6.

13 A palanquin is a litter for one, borne on poles carried on men's shoulders. Emily Eden (1797–1869) writing of her travels in India described the palanquin as 'nothing but a bed in a box'. *Tigers, Durbars and Kings, Fanny Eden's Indian Journals, 1837–1838*, Janet Dunbar and John Murray (eds.), 1988, p. xiv.

14 *East Indian Register and Directory*, Births, Deaths and Marriages, 1838.

15 Mackenzie, *op cit.*, 1852, p. 6.

16 Meg Gomersall, *Working-Class Girls in Nineteenth Century England – Life, Work and Schooling*, MacMillan Press, Ltd, Basingstoke and London, 1997, p. 106.

17 Lieutenant General Sir Frederick Adams was Governor of Madras from 1832–37.

18 Eneas Mackenzie, *Memoirs* and *Emigrant's Guide.*

19 Eneas Mackenzie, *Memoirs*, p. 21.

20 *Military Consultation*, vol. 1258, the Tamil Nadu Archives, Egmore, Madras.

Australia and Emigration 1838–1846

1 Joanna Trollope, *Britannia's Daughters – Women of the British Empire*, Pimlico, 1994, p. 18; first published Hutchinson, 1983.

2 *Ibid.*, p. 21.

3 Edward W. Said, *Culture & Imperialism*, Chatto & Windus, London, 1993, p. xvi.

4 Robin F. Haines, *Emigration and the Labouring Poor – Australian Recruitment in Britain and Ireland, 1831–1860*, Macmillan Press Ltd, Basingstoke, 1997; first published USA, St Martin's Press Inc, 1997, p. 2.

5 *Ibid.*, p. 85.

6 *Ibid.*, pp. 79–80.

7 *Ibid.*, p. 17.

8 *Ibid.*, p. 9.

9 Alan Brissenden and Charles Higham, *They Came to Australia, An Anthology*, Angus & Robertson, London, 1962, p. 19.

10 *The Journal of John Dickson Loch, 1837–39, passenger on the Emerald Isle*, (quoted Margaret Kiddle, 1957, p. 4). The journal was in the possession of Mrs Evelyn Snodgrass c.1950 when Kiddle was writing her thesis/biography.

11 Report, Select Committee of the Legislative Council, appointed 8 November 1843. 'To take into consideration a Petition from upwards of 4,000 of the Inhabitants of Sydney, soliciting the attention of the Council to the distressed Condition of the numerous unemployed Artisans and Labourers in the City of Sydney, having accordingly taken the same into Consideration, and examined various Witnesses, both as to the actual Condition of the Unemployed in Sydney, and the demand for Labour of various kinds in the Interior'. Irish University Press, British Parliamentary Papers, Colonies, Australia 7, 1842–44, p. 522.

12 *Ibid.*

13 Marjorie Barnard, *Sydney – The Story of a City*, Melbourne University Press; London and New York, Cambridge University Press, 1956, p. 26.

14 A letter from the Colonial Secretary's Office, Sydney, 28 October 1835 set out the Notice Introducing the Bounty System. Copies of Correspondence Respecting Emigration, 64. British Parliamentary Papers, 1837, XLIII, p. 358. The regulations were changed in 1837 and 1840. The new regulations were published in the *New South Wales Government Gazette* on 25 September 1837 and 18 March 1840.

15 William Walker, *Reminiscences (Personal, Social and Political) of a Fifty Years' Residence at Windsor, on the Hawkesbury*, Turner and Henderson, Sydney. Facsimile reprint 1997, p. 6; first published 1890.

16 G. Donaldson, *The Scots Overseas*, London, 1966, p. 20.

17 J. Steel, *Early Days of Windsor*, Library of Australian History, 1977; first published 1916, p. 122.

18 William Walker, *op cit.*, p. 11.

19 *Ibid.*, p. 10.

20 Parkes overcame his dislike of wicked Australia. He went on to be the Premier of NSW on five occasions between 1872 and 1891. He was knighted in 1877. Ruth Teale, *Colonial Eve – Sources on Women in Australia, 1788–1914*, Melbourne University Press, 1978, p. 49.

21 Maurice Bruce, *The Coming of the Welfare State*, Batsford Ltd, London, 1978, p. 89. First published 1961.

22 Dora Peyser, *Royal Australian Historical Society Journal and Proceedings*, Vol. XXV, 1939, part 110, p. 109.

23 *Ibid.*

24 *Ibid.*

25 *Ibid.* It was due to Elizabeth Fry's influence that a barrack for the female convicts was built at Parramatta, and a Ladies Committee established. According to reports that came in the 1830s, however, the situation in Parramatta had deteriorated considerably. Annemicke van Drenth & Francisca de Haan, *The Rise of Caring Power – Elizabeth Fry and Josephine Butler in Britain and the Netherlands*, Amsterdam University Press, 1999, p. 59.

26 Samuel Sidney, *The Three Colonies of Australia; New South Wales, Victoria, South Australia; Their Pastures, Copper Mines, & Gold Fields*, Ingram, Cooke and Co, London, 1853, p. 34.

27 *Ibid.*

28 Caroline Chisholm, *Female Immigration*, 1842, p. 1.

29 *Ibid.*, p. 2.

30 *Ibid.*

31 Eneas Mackenie, *Memoirs*, 1853, p. 23.

32 Kiddle writes that Captain Chisholm was recalled to active service in the Chinese 'Opium War', but there is nothing within his service record to suggest that this was the case. *Op cit.*, 1957, p. 5.

33 General Orders, 24 November 1840, British Library, 1/Mill/11/41, 375.

34 Twenty-three years' service in India with three years' furlough would have enabled Archibald to retire on a Captain's pay of £191.12s.6d. per annum, but by prudently remaining in India a further four years he was entitled to retire on a Major's pay at £292 per annum. As the Chisholms were not financially secure the difference in pay would have been a significant consideration. *The Calendar for the year 1846*, p. 193, supplied by Tamil Nadu Archives, India.

35 Eneas Mackenzie, *Memoirs*, 1853, p. 23.

36 Samuel Sidney, *op cit.*, p. 34.

37 See particularly Helen Heney, *Caroline Chisholm – Pioneer Social Worker*, paper read before the RAHS, 29 September 1942 and published in their Journal, V. 29, 1943, pp. 21–34.

38 Caroline Chisholm, *Female Emigration*, 1842, p. 3.

39 *Ibid.*, p. 2.

40 *Ibid.*, p. 4.

41 T. R. Luscombe, 'Caroline Chisholm – Keeper of the National Conscience' in *Builders and Crusaders*, 1967, p. 510.

42 Caroline Chisholm, *Female Immigration*, 1842, p. 6.

43 Letter from Fr. Brennan of Sydney printed in *The Chronicle*, 16 September 1841.

44 Caroline Chisholm, *Female Immigration*, p. 6.

45 *Ibid.*

46 *Ibid.*

47 *Chronicle*, 16 September 1841.

48 Caroline Chisholm, *Female Immigration*, pp. 8–9

49 *Ibid.*, p. 10.

50 *Ibid.*, pp. 10, 11.

51 Samuel Sidney, *The Three Colonies of Australia*, 1853, p. 136.

52 Joan Perkin, *Victorian Women*, John Murray, London, 1993, p. 236.

53 Miriam Dixson, *The Real Matilda, Women and Identity in Australia 1788 to the Present*; revised edition, Penguin Books, Australia, 1987, pp. 96, 289; first published 1972.

54 Eve Pownall, *Mary of Maranoa - Tales of Australian Pioneer Women*, F. H. Johnston, Sydney, 1964, p. 140; first published in 1959.
55 *Ibid.*, p. 151.
56 Mrs Charles Clacy, *A Lady's Visit to the Gold Diggings of Australia in 1842–53 – written on the spot by Mrs Charles Clacy*, Patricia Thompson (ed.), Angus & Robertson, London, 1962, p. 151; first published 1853.
57 See Norris Pope, *Dickens and Charity*, Macmillan, 1978 and chapter 4, Edna Healey, *Lady Unknown – The Life of Angela Burdett-Coutts*, Sidgwick & Jackson, 1978.
58 *Argus*, Melbourne, 17 February 1855.
59 *Northampton Mercury*, 5 March 1853.
60 R. Dalziel, 'The Colonial Helpmeet – Women's Role and Vote in 19th Century New Zealand' in *New Zealand Journal of History*, vol. II, no. 2, October 1977.
61 Caroline Chisholm, *Female Emigration*, 1842, pp. 86/87.
62 *Ibid.*, p. 75.
63 *Ibid.*, p. 62.
64 *Ibid.*, p. 86.
65 *Ibid.*, pp. 69, 70.
66 *Ibid.*, pp. 13–17.
67 William Joy, *The Venturers*, Shakespeare Head Press, Sydney, 1972, p. 72.
68 *Ibid.*, p. 73.
69 *Ibid.*, p. 72.
70 *Ibid.*, p. 75.
71 British Parliamentary Papers, Irish University Press, *Colonies*, Australia, 7, Sessions, 1842–44, p. 543.
72 Margaret Kiddle, *Caroline Chisholm*, Melbourne University Press, 1957, p. 52.
73 V&P Legislative Committee, 1844, Report, Committee on Distressed Labourers.
74 Mary Hoban, *Caroline Chisholm*, 1984, p. 152.
75 BPP, IUP, Colonies, Australia, 9, pp. 723–30.
76 Caroline was referring to Rule No. 3 of the then current regulations whereby young women were required to be assigned to the charge of a family. Caroline suggested that many of the women travelling in this manner did not meet with the family who were to act as her protectors until the ship was about to leave port.
77 Haines, *op cit.*, Appendix 4, p. 272.
78 G. F. Plant, *Overseas Settlement*, Royal Institute of International Affairs, p. 38. Undated c1949.

79 Haines, *op cit.*, p. 273.

80 *Ibid.*, p. 274.

81 *Ibid.*, p. 275.

82 Caroline Chisholm, *Female Immigration*, p. 19.

83 *Ibid.*, pp. 23–30.

84 The 'Nineteen Counties' of white settlement were Argyle, Bathurst, Bligh, Brisbane, Camden, Cook, Cumberland, Durham, Georgiana, Gloucester, Hunter, King, Murray, Northumberland, Phillip, Roxburgh, St Vincent, Wellington and Westmoreland.

85 The *Empire*, 11 December 1860.

86 *Sydney Morning Herald*, 14 May 1846.

87 *Sydney Morning Herald*, 20 March 1846. Caroline Chisholm's letter to 'The Colonists of NSW'.

88 *Australian Dictionary of Biography*, Melbourne University Publishing, 1967, vol. 2, p. 77–8.

89 *Ibid.*

90 John Dunmore Lane, *Transportation and Colonization, or the Causes of the comparative failure of the transportation system in the Australian Colonies; with suggestions for ensuring its future efficiency in subserviency to extensive colonization*, 1837. Statistics compiled of the approximate 123,000 men and 25,000 women who were transported to New South Wales and Van Diemen's Land (and of whom 1.8 per cent had died on the voyage out) one-third were Roman Catholic and two-thirds were Protestants. L. L. Robson, *The Convict Settlers of Australia*, Melbourne University Press, 1994, p. 8.

91 John Dunmore Lane, *The Question of Questions, or is this Colony to be transformed into a Province of the Popedom? A letter to the Protestant landholders of New South Wales*, 1841.

92 R. B. Madgwick, *Immigration into Eastern Australia 1788–1851*, Sydney University Press, 1969, p. 234; first published 1937.

93 A reference to Lord Clarendon, the Lord-Lieutenant of Ireland, who, with Earl Grey, was accused of being Mrs Chisholm's dupe. *British Banner*, 21 November 1849, p. 739.

94 Eneas Mackenzie, *Memoirs*, pp. 82–3.

95 Statistics compiled from Haines (p. 261) show that just over 26,000 emigrants arrived in New South Wales between 1841 and 1846 (from the foundation of Caroline's Home and her departure for Britain). Not all of those immigrants would have required help; some would have had friends and/or relatives and jobs to go to. That Caroline placed nearly 11,000 immigrants (almost half of those who arrived in the colony during this time) in employment is no little achievement.

96 Caroline Chisholm, *Female Immigration*, 1842, p. viii. Hoban notes (1984, p. 95) that a book by 'a Lady long resident in New South Wales' entitled *A Mother's Offering to her Children*, was published in 1841. The book was dedicated to the son of Sir George and Lady Gipps, and was, its author claimed, 'the first work written in the Colony expressly for Children'. Either Caroline was not aware of the publication of this work, or had discounted it because it was a children's book that recounted accounts of shipwrecks drawn from printed sources.

97 *Sydney Morning Herald*, 3 April 1850.

98 G. Elliot Anstruther, *Caroline Chisholm The Emigrants' Friend*, Catholic Truth Society, 1916, pp. 14, 15.

99 *Ibid.*

100 *Ibid.*

England and Emigration 1846–1854

1 Edith Pearson, *Ideals and Realities*, 1914, p. 82.

2 Colonial Land and Emigration Commissioners, NSW, 1847, *General Report*, pp. 7–10.

3 Archives Authority of NSW, 2135 Agent's Lists.

4 23 October 1847, No. 67, 1333.

5 B. Harris, *What has Mrs Caroline Chisholm done for the Colony of New South Wales?*, 1862, p. 4.

6 Mary Hoban, *Caroline Chisholm – A Biography*, 1984, p. 202.

7 *Ibid.*, pp. 202–3.

8 Caroline Chisholm, *Emigration and Transportation Relatively Considered*, 1847, p. 3.

9 *Ibid.*

10 *Ibid.*

11 *Ibid.*

12 *Ibid.*

13 *Ibid.*, p. 9.

14 *Sydney Morning Herald*, 11 December 1860.

15 *Ibid.*, 4 April 1847.

16 Charlton Crescent is now Charlton Place. Number 3 has a blue plaque giving details of Caroline Chisholm's residence there.

17 Wiltshire Record Office, WRO 2057/F8/VIII 260.

18 House of Lords, Select Committee on Colonization from Ireland, Third Report, pp. 407–24.

19 From Caroline's letter to a 'gentleman' in Sydney from the family home at 29 Prince Street, Jubilee Place, Commercial Road, London, dated 30 November 1846 and published in the *Sydney Morning Herald* on 5 April 1847.

20 Caroline Chisholm, *The A.B.C. of Colonization*, 1850, p. 2.

21 *Ibid.*, p. 10.

22 Ellen Layton, 'On Superintendence of Female Emigrants' read at the Social Science Congress in Edinburgh. *Transactions of the National Association for the Promotion of Social Science*, 1864, pp. 616–18.

23 Trowbridge Record Office, WRO 2057/F8/viii 39(a).

24 Caroline Chisholm, *FCLS* pamphlet, 1849.

25 The dedication was to Lord Ashley. Anthony Ashley Cooper was the eldest son of the sixth Earl of Shaftesbury. He took the title Lord Ashley in 1811 when his father became a peer, and became Lord Shaftesbury when he succeeded his father in 1851.

26 *Chamber's Edinburgh Journal*, 15 October 1853, p. 243.

27 B. and J. L. Hammond, *Lord Shaftesbury*, 1969, p. 5.

28 Georgina Battiscombe, *Shaftesbury, a Biography of the Seventh Earl 1801–1855*, 1974, p. 206, wrote, 'Most of the boys went to Australia, in later years [after 1848] girls were more often sent to Canada under the auspices of a Miss Chisholm, a Roman Catholic lady whose co-operation with him called down upon Ashley's head the wrath of his more bigoted fellow Protestants.'

29 *The Times*, 10 August 1853.

30 *Empire*, 14 June 1861.

31 *The Times*, 29 September 1851.

32 *Illustrated London News*, 28 February 1852.

33 A. James Hammerton, *Emigrant Gentlewomen – Genteel Poverty and Female Emigration 1830–1914*, 1979, pp. 97–9.

34 Wiltshire Record Office, WRO 2057/F8/VIII 27.

35 A Barque, or Bark, is a vessel with three masts, square rigged at her fore and main masts like a ship, but differs from a ship in that it has no top at her mizzen-mast, and carries only fore-and-aft sails on that mast.

36 Detail from the *Log of Voyage from London to Port Phillip, per Barque 'Slains Castle' September 1850 to January 1851*, by A. L. Whitby. I am grateful to Mr Allan Hillier of Melbourne, Australia, for allowing me to have a copy of the log and to quote from it.

37 B. Harris, *What has Mrs Caroline Chisholm done…*, 1862, p. 181.

38 *Cork Southern Reporter*, 1 May 1852.

39 Eneas Mackenzie, *Memoirs*, 1852, pp. 175–7.
40 Margaret Kiddle, 1957, p. 151.
41 *Illustrated London News*, 28 February 1852.
42 *Illustrated London News*, 10 May 1851.
43 See Afterword for further details of Samuel Sidney.
44 *The Morning Chronicle*, 23 September 1851; *The Times*, 29 September 1851.
45 Eneas Mackenzie, *Memoirs*, p. 183.
46 *Ibid.*, p. 184.
47 Wiltshire Records Office, Trowbridge, WRO, 2057/F8.VIII 3 (c).
48 *Ibid.*, WRO 2057/F8.VIII 5.
49 *Illustrated London News*, 28 February 1852.
50 Public Record Office of Victoria website, under 'Unassisted Immigration to Victoria'.
51 See the Ballarat genealogy website and Jan Bassett, *The Concise Oxford Dictionary of Australian History*, 1986.
52 Presumably Mr Elgot was referring to Archibald junior who would have been about sixteen in 1852. Archibald was the eldest son born in India in 1836.
53 Public Record Office of Victoria, as above.
54 Margaret Kiddle, 1957, Appendix F, quoting Passenger List at the Public Library of Victoria, Melbourne.
55 *Hebrew Observer*, 24 June 1853.
56 Eneas Mackenzie, *Emigrant's Guide*, p. 25.
57 Robin F Haines, *Emigration and the Labouring Poor, Australian Recruitment in Britain and Ireland, 1831–60*, 1997, p. 217, note 82; p. 357.
58 My sincere thanks to Dr Audrey Carpenter who, when visiting Sydney, researched the shipping files at the Archives Authority of NSW. (Cash from Family Colonization Loan Society's Immigrants pp. 30–2.)
59 National Library of Australia, *NLA News*, May 2001, vol. XI, no. 8.
60 Eneas Mackenzie, *Memoirs*, 1852, pp. 27–8.
61 B. Harris, 1862, p. 8.
62 Trowbridge Record Office, papers of Sir Sydney Herbert, WRO 2057/F8/VIII 4.
63 House of Commons, Select Committee on Emigrant Ships, First Report, Minutes of Evidence, Proceedings, Appendix and Index.
64 *Ibid.*
65 Cecil Woodham-Smith, *Florence Nightingale*, Constable, 1992, p. 295.
66 W. H. Wills ('Chips') *Household Words*, vol. III, 31 May 1851.

67 Norris Pope, *Dickens and Charity*, 1978, p. 10.

68 Dickens was involved with the planning and launching of Urania Cottage in 1846–47. He continued to be involved with the cottage until 1858.

69 Edna Healey, *Coutts & Co, 1692–1992 – The Portrait of a Private Bank*, 1992, p. 311.

70 *Ibid.*

71 Anne Lohrili, *Household Words – A Weekly Journal 1850–1859 Conducted by Charles Dickens*, 1973, pp. 226–7.

72 Richard Henry Horne (Hengist) contributed articles to more than fifty periodicals—British, Australian and American. He wrote poetry, poetic dramas and books and was involved with *Household Words* from the beginning. *Household Words*, 1, 22 June 1850, pp. 307–10.

73 *Household Words*, 1, 30 March 1850, p. 24; Lohrli, *Household Words*, 1973.

74 *Household Narrative* was published monthly during 1850. Because of financial difficulties it ceased publication at the end of 1850. Articles concerning Caroline appeared in January, pp. 18–19; May, p. 116; June, p. 140; July, p. 165; and October, p. 235.

75 Charles Dickens, *Bleak House*, chapter IV, 1852–53.

76 Lohrli, *Household Words*, p. 227.

77 Healey, *Coutts & Co*, p. 98.

78 Peter Ackroyd, *Dickens*, 1990, p. 586.

79 Pope, *Dickens and Charity*, p. 186.

80 *Illustrated Magazine of Art*, vol. II, 1854, 178.

81 Margaret Kiddle, 1957, p. 166.

82 Anne Lohrli suggests that Harriet Martineau, who was also a *Household Words* contributor, was generally credited in contemporary reports as being Mrs Jellyby's original.

83 Mary Jane Kinnaird (née Hoare) was one of Victorian England's leading evangelical women. She particularly supported the Biblewomen's Mission, the Christian Colportage Association, the Foreign Aid Society, the Foreign Evangelisation Society, the Waldensian Mission (in Italy), the Calvin Memorial Hall (in Geneva), the Zenana Bible and Medical Mission (in India), the Indian Female Normal School and Instruction Society, the Prayer Union and the YWCA (of which Mrs Kinnaird was effectively a co-founder). Mrs Kinnaird's biographer felt called upon to disclaim the Mrs Jellyby image, and to stress that Mrs Kinnaird was no less attentive to her domestic responsibilities. Pope, 1978, pp. 245–6.

84 Lohrli, *Household Words*, p. 227, and Pope, *Dickens and Charity*, p. 246.

85 Kiddle, 1957, p. 169.

86 Ackroyd, *Dickens*, p. 456.

87 A chronological list of the 'Q' papers can be found in the appendix to the article 'Douglas Jerrold's "Q" Papers in *Punch*', by Bruce A. White, *Victorian Periodicals Review*, vol. XV, no. 4, Winter 1982, p. 137.

88 Caroline's articles appear under her name with the title of 'Home in the Bush – Advice to Emigrants'. They date from 23 October 1847 to 2 February 1848.

89 *Punch*, vol. iv, no. 81, 28 January 1843, p. 46.

90 'Q', *Punch* vol. II, no. 45, 21 May 1842, p. 210.

91 F. C. Mather, *Chartism and Society – An Anthology of Documents*, 1980, pp. 128–30.

92 Kathryn Gleadle, *The Early Feminists: Radical Unitarians and the Emergence of the Women's Rights Movement, 1831–51*, 1995, p. 44.

93 *Douglas Jerrold's Weekly Newspaper*, no. 63, October 1847, p. 1336.

94 Michael Slater, Professor of Victorian Literature at Birkbeck College, University of London, has published a new biography of Jerrold: *Douglas Jerrold, 1803–1857*, Duckworth, 2002. He has found no mention of Caroline in any of the Jerrold letters he has examined in libraries both here and in the USA. He has not found any mention of her in any other works on Jerrold, other than the reference in Walter Jerrold's biography. My thanks to Professor Slater for his help.

95 *Illustrated London News*, 15 April 1854, p. 337.

96 Walter Jerrold, *Douglas Jerrold, Dramatist and Wit*, 1919, p. 601.

97 The *Herald* and *Empire* no doubt refer to the *Sydney Morning Herald* and the Sydney paper the *Empire*. *Chambers' Journal* would be the *Chambers' Edinburgh Journal*, price 1½d. The journal was conducted by William and Robert Chambers, also editors of *Chambers' Information for the People*, and *Chambers' Educational Course*, etc. The paper was of liberal persuasion. The *Chambers' Edinburgh Journal* carried articles on Chisholm on 30 March 1850, 25 September 1852 and 15 October 1853. Dickens' *Household Words* was also liberal in viewpoint, and, as noted, supported Caroline's work. *Lloyds Weekly London Newspaper* was more radical and sensational in style.

98 John Moran (ed.), *Little Joe*, 1991, pp. 75–6.

99 Present research has established that Caroline spoke at thirty-two lectures/talks/ emigration meetings between April 1850 and April 1854. Undoubtedly there were others. During this time Caroline gave birth to two daughters: Sarah, born January, but died in August 1850, and Harriet Monica, born July 1851.

100 MS 8994/26, by courtesy of the Librarian, Wellcome Institute for the History of Medicine

101 Wellcome Institute, MS 8994/76.

102 *The Times*, 10 August 1853.

103 Hoban, *Caroline Chisholm*, 1984, p. 322.

104 Sedgley Park School, near Wolverhampton. The school was founded in 1763 mainly for the middle classes, but gentry did send their boys to the school—all were treated the same. The purpose of the school was not to produce priests, although many were later ordained as such; it was to give a good faith-based education to England's middle class and prepare them for life as good Catholics, in whatever walk of life they chose. Geography, arithmetic and handwriting were offered as a basic. Arithmetic combined book-keeping and land measuring, very useful to a future in commerce. Drawing, music, dancing, singing, deportment and elocution were also part of the curriculum, as was sport. Details from the Sedgley Park website.

105 Cardinal Fransoni was Prefect of Propaganda College, Rome, from 1834 until 1856.

106 Caroline went to Ireland in May 1852.

107 Birmingham Archdiocesan Archives, Ref: R502, archived with the date 1874. Bishop Ullathorne was Bishop of Birmingham from 1850 until 1888. Caroline would have known him from his time in Australia. Ullathorne was in Windsor, Australia at the time the Chisholm family was there.

108 Detail from Sedgley Park website, above.

109 Kiddle, 1957, p. 171.

110 Archibald Chisholm, letter in the *Belfast Gazette*, [Port Fairy] Australia, 1851.

111 Kiddle, 1957, p. 172.

112 *Ibid.*, p. 176.

113 Keith Pescod, *A Place to Lay My Head: Immigrant Shelters of Nineteenth Century Victoria*, Australian Scholarly Publishing, Melbourne, 2003, p. 102.

114 Kiddle, 1957, p. 176.

115 *Ibid.*, p. 102–3.

116 The story of Thomas Lyle and family from England, their voyage to Melbourne in 1842, by kind permission of Dione Coumbe.

117 Kiddle, 1957, p. 180–1.

118 *Ibid.*, p. 163.

119 Hoban, *Caroline Chisholm*, 1984, p. 281.

120 La Trobe Library, MS6318.

121 *c.*1833–1854 32 CY2097-ZAC19/1ML AC 19-A/1-10.

122 John Cassell, *Illustrated Magazine of Art*, 1854, vol. II, p. 177.

123 Robin F. Haines, *Emigration and the Labouring* Poor, 1997, pp. 261–3.

124 Kiddle, 1957, p. 195.

125 Cassell, *Illustrated Magazine of Art*, 1852; Mackenzie, *Emigrant's Guide*, 1852, p. 25.

Australia Revisited 1854–1866, & Again in Britain 1866–1877

1 W. P. Morrell, *The Gold Rushes*, Adam and Charles Black, London, 1968, p, 200; first published 1936.
2 *Ibid.*, p. 202.
3 *Ibid.*, p. 209.
4 *Ibid.*
5 *Ibid.*, p. 210.
6 Margaret Kiddle, *Caroline Chisholm*, p. 246–7.
7 Miscellaneous Papers re Caroline Chisholm *c.*1833–1854 – State Library of New South Wales: 32 CY2097-ZAC19/1-2 ML AC 19-A/1-10.
8 Kiddle, 1957, pp. 202–6.
9 Mary Hoban, *Caroline Chisholm*, p. 331.
10 Brenda Stevens-Chambers, *Friend and Foe: Caroline Chisholm and the Women of Kyneton, 1840–2004*, Springfield & Hart, 2004, p. 331.
11 Mary Hoban, as above, p. 354.
12 Brenda Stevens-Chambers, as above, p. 27.
13 *Ibid.*, p. 16.
14 *Ibid.*, p. 19.
15 *Ibid.*, p. 20.
16 Elizabeth Roberts, *Women's Work 1840–1940*, Macmillan, 1990, p. 37; first published 1988.
17 John Moran, *Little Joe*; first published in the *Empire*, 26 December 1859 to 15 May 1860; reprinted in one volume by John Moran, Preferential Publications, Ashgrove, Australia, 1991, p. 52.
18 *Ibid.*, p. 53. Interestingly Hoban comments (without notation) that 'in the store they [the Chisholms] found that old blue willow-pattern china would not sell; that pickles, wines and spirits sold according to the bottles, and shirts and gloves to the boxing'. Hoban, 1984, p. 368.
19 Moran, 1991, p. 77.
20 William Howitt, *Land, Labour and Gold or Two Years in Victoria, with Visits to Sydney and Van Diemen's Land*, Lowden Publishing Company, Kilmore, Australia, 1972, p. 336; first published 1855 by Longman, Brown, Green and Longmans.
21 *Ibid.*, p. 340.
22 *Ibid.*, p. 341.

23 The Eureka Rebellion was an armed conflict in 1854 between diggers and government authorities on the goldfields at Ballarat, Victoria. The diggers' grievances included the licence system and its administration, for which the diggers were forced to pay thirty shillings a month. The miners had to carry their licences at all times and had to face licence hunts, which were deeply resented. There was corruption among officials, and the diggers had no political representation and only limited access to land. A Royal Commission was appointed in 1854 to inquire into the state of the goldfields. Its recommendations, most of which were adopted, included the abolition of the licence fee, the introduction of an export duty on gold and the introduction of a miner's right, which conferred legal and political rights, to cost £1 a year.

24 Kiddle, 1957, pp. 220–5.

25 Keith Pescod, *A Place to Lay My Head, Immigrant Shelters of Nineteenth Century Victoria*, Australian Scholarly Publishing, 2003, Appendix L, p. 170.

26 Details from a facsimile poster, the original of which was published in the 1850s and preserved in an album of cuttings and souvenirs kept by the Chisholm family. Purhased by Hoban in Tasmania, 1976, and now at the Immigration Museum in Melbourne. The poster was reprinted by kind permission of *The Age* for the Caroline Chisholm Society, a voluntary family welfare organisation which tries to emulate in the modern world the spirit of Caroline Chisholm.

27 *The Argus*, 13 June 1857.

28 Eneas Mackenzie was still publishing books in England in 1855. There is no record of him in England in the 1861 census. Australian registers show that Eneas Mackenzie died in Victoria in 1865, aged 57. His wife, Sarah Mackenzie (née Dockling) died in Victoria in 1866, aged 58. Records indicate that the children of Eneas and Sarah Mackenzie were resident in Victoria. My thanks to Dr John and Dr Audrey Carpenter for their assistance.

29 Brenda Stevens-Chambers, as above, p. 24, quoting *The Argus*, 1857.

30 *Ibid.*, p. 25.

31 B. Harris, *What has Mrs Caroline Chisholm done for the Colony of New South Wales?*, James Cole, Sydney, 1862, p. 14.

32 Reported in the *Empire*, 9 September 1859, and *Sydney Morning Herald*, 9 September 1859. All quotations concerning the lecture are taken from these articles. This and the three other lectures have been ably put together in one volume by John Moran under the title of *Radical, in Bonnet and Shawl, Four Political Lectures by Caroline Chisholm*, Preferential Publications, 1994, pp. 13–40.

33 Premier Charles Cowper and the Lands Minister. See Moran, as above, p. 30.

34 See the *Empire*, 11 December 1860; *Sydney Morning Herald*, 11 December 1860 and *Freeman's Journal*, 12 December 1860. See also Moran, as above, pp. 41–72.

35 John Moran, as above, p. 67.

36 *Freeman's Journal*, 23 February 1861; *Sydney Morning Herald*, Friday 22 February 1861. See also Moran, as above, pp. 73–86.

37 Moran, as above, p. 83.

38 The *Empire*, 14 June 1861; *Freeman's Journal*, 15 June 1861 and the *Sydney Morning Herald*, 14 June 1861. See also John Moran as above, pp. 87–116.

39 *Ibid.*

40 *Ibid.*, John Moran, p. 108.

41 The *Empire*, 14 June 1861; *Freeman's Journal*, 15 June 1861 and the *Sydney Morning Herald*, 14 June 1861. See also John Moran as above, pp. 87–116.

42 The *Empire*, Chapter 1, 26 December 1859; chapter 2, 30 December 1859; chapter 3, 6 January 1860; chapter 4, 18 January 1860; chapter 5, 6 February 1860; chapter 6, 14 February1860; chapter 7, 27 February 1860; chapter 8, 5 March 1860; chapter 9, 8 March 1860; chapter 10; 23 April 1860 and chapter 11, 15 May 1860. See also John Moran, ed., *Little Joe*, by Caroline Chisholm, Preferential Publications, 1991.

43 Hoban, 1984, p. 390.

44 *Ibid.*, p. 391.

45 Detail from the diaries of Elizabeth Rathbone, Liverpool University, Sydney Jones Library, RPVI.l.477 and 478.

46 Colonel John Chisholm, 31 Clarence Square, Cheltenham.

47 The information was kindly supplied by Sister Jessica Leonard S.M. of the Marist Sisters. She has made an historical study of the Marist Sisters' archives in relation to their foundations in England, including Highgate, 1863–70.

48 Margaret Kiddle, 1957, p. 232.

49 Liverpool University, Sydney Jones Library, RPVI.1477.

50 Liverpool University, Sydney Jones Library, RPVI.1.477.

51 Liverpool University, Sydney Jones Library RPVI.1.478.

52 Hoban, 1984, pp. 410–12.

53 *Ibid.*, p. 416.

54 *Ibid.*

55 Wellcome Institute, Florence Nightingale Letter, Easter Day 1977–1 April 1977.

Afterword

1 Anne Lohrli, *Household Words – A Weekly Journal 1850–1859*. Conducted by Charles Dickens, University of Toronto Press, 1973, pp. 420–3.

2 Alan Brissenden, and Charles Higham, *They Came to Australia, An Anthology*, Angus and Robertson, London, 1962, p. 15. Robin F. Haines, *Emigration and the Labouring Poor – Australian Recruitment in Britain and Ireland, 1831–60*, Macmillan Press Ltd, Basingstoke, 1997, pp. 170/71, 179/80, 339 n17; first published USA, St Martin's Press, Inc, 1997.

3 Samuel Sidney, *Emigrant's Journal and Traveller's Magazine*, August 1849, pp. 285/6.

4 J. and M. Collingwood, *Hannah More*, Lion Paperback, Oxford and Sydney, 1990, p. 77.

5 Sidney's *Journal*, as above, p. 286.

6 Margaret Swann, 'Caroline Chisholm', *Journal of the Royal Australia Historical Society*, vol. vi, Part 2, 1925, p. 9.

7 Margaret Kiddle, *Caroline Chisholm*, Melbourne University Press, 1957, p. 5; first published 1950; abridged edition, 1969; reprinted with Introduction by Patricia Grimshaw, 1990.

8 Mary Hoban, *Caroline Chisholm etc.*, 1984, p. 26/27.

9 Joanna Bogle, *Caroline Chisholm: The Emigrant's Friend*, Gracewing, Fowler Wright Books, Herefordshire, England, 1993, p. 46.

10 *ILN*, 15 April 1854, p. 337.

11 Samuel Sidney, *The Three Colonies of Australia*, 1853, p. iii.

12 *ILN*, 10 May 1851, p. 378.

13 Sidney, *Three Colonies*, as above, pp. ii/iii.

14 *Ibid.*, p. iii.

15 C. J. Hunt, *The Book Trade in Northumberland and Durham to 1860*, Thornes' Students' Bookshops' Ltd, 1975, p. 63. Northern Tribune, 1854, Vol. 1, 191.

16 Hunt, as above, pp. 114/119.

17 J. Knott, *Circulating Libraries in Newcastle in the Eighteenth and Nineteenth Centuries. Library History*, vol. 2, no. 6, Autumn 1972, p. 244.

18 Hunt, as above, pp. 63/64.

19 Joan Perkin, *Victorian Women*, John Murray, London, 1993, p. 6.

20 Lucasta Miller, *The Brontë Myth*, Jonathan Cape, London, 2001, p. 81.

21 Mackenzie, *The Emigrant's Guide to Australia with Memoir of Mrs Chisholm*, Clarke, Beeton & Co, London, 1853, p. 4.

22 *Ibid.*, p. ix.

23 Mary Hoban, *Caroline Chisholm etc.*, 1984, p. 244.

24 Mackenzie, *Memoirs*, Preface, p. viii.

25 *Ibid.*, p. v.

26 Millar, as above, pp. 81/82.

27 Samuel Smiles, *Self-Help; with Illustrations of Conduct and Perseverance*, John Murray, London, 1880, pp. 365/366.

28 Trelawney Saunders, *The Story of the Life of Mrs Caroline Chisholm, The Emigrants' Friend, and her Adventures in Australia*, 1852, p. 1.

29 Millar, as above, p. 244.

30 Rodney Stinson, published in Sydney by Yorkcross Pty Ltd, 2008, p. 157.

31 The Catholic Press, Sydney, New South Wales, 9 September 1909, written under the pseudonym Arrah Luen; *The Influence of Women, A Lecture Delivered by Miss Fitzsimmons, Chairman of the Catholic Women's League*, Manchester, 16 June 1909, and *The Tablet*, London, Saturday, 19 June 1909. See Stinson, as above, p. 157.

32 Stinson, see above, p. 157.

33 Edith Pearson, *Ideals and Realities – Essays*, R. T. Washbourne Ltd, London, 1914, pp. 1 and 71.

34 Margaret Kiddle, *Caroline Chisholm*, Melbourne University Press, 1957 (first published 1950); abridged edition, 1969; reprinted with Introduction by Patricia Grimshaw, 1990, p. xxvii.

35 Anstruther, 1916, p. 4.

36 The eminent French historian and author Jules Michelet devoted a chapter on Caroline in his book *La Femme*, Paris, 1862, 657ff, (translation). Michelet wrote that 'the fifth part of the world, Australia, has up to now but one saint, one legend … The richest and most powerful government in the world … failed in colonization … where a simple woman succeeded by her force of character and her vigour of soul'.

37 Grimshaw, in Kiddle, as above, p. xxviii.

38 Margaret Swann, *Caroline Chisholm, Friend to the Unemployed and Migrants*, New South Wales and Victoria, 1838–66, Sydney, 1925, p. 1.

39 *Ibid.*, p. 2.

40 *Ibid.*, p. 17.

41 *Ibid.*, p. 54.

42 *Ibid.*, p. 47.

43 Flora Eldershaw, *The Peaceful Army*, ed. Dale Spender, Penguin Books, Penguin Australia Women's Library, 1988, p. 161.

44 *Ibid.*, p. vii.

45 *Ibid.*, p. 57.

46 *Ibid.*, p. 55.

47 Anne Summers, *Damned Whores and God's Police*, revised edition, Ringwood, Australia, Penguin, 1994, p. 63; first published Allen Lane, Australia, 1975.

48 Patricia Grimshaw wrote an Introduction to the reprint of Margaret Kiddle's book in 1990, p. xxxii.

49 *Ibid.*, p. xxix. Sir Keith Hancock was an eminent Australian historian whose history of Australia appeared in print in Sydney in 1945 (Kiddle, 1957, pp. 236–47).

50 *Ibid.*, p. xxxii.

51 *Northampton Mercury*, 5 March 1853.

52 Kiddle, as above, pp. xxx, xxxi.

53 Mary Hoban, *Caroline Chisholm – A Biography, Fifty-one Pieces of Wedding Cake*, The Polding Press, Mebourne, 1984, p. ix.

54 Kiddle, as above, 1990, p. xxxiii.

55 *Ibid.*

56 Mary Hoban, as above, p. 5.

57 *Pigot's Directory* for 1824 and 1830.

58 Carole Walker, 'Setting the Record Straight: Caroline Chisholm, née Jones, 1808–1877, The Early Years – Northampton', in *Northamptonshire Past and Present,* Number 56, 2003, pages 177-91.

59 Joanna Bogle, *Caroline Chisholm: The Emigrant's Friend*, Gracewing, Fowler Wright Books, Herefordshire, England, 1993, p. 154.

60 Robert sold the land *c.*1821 following his marriage and twenty-first birthday and just prior to his emigration to America. No documentation has been found to suggest that Caroline actually received her inheritance.

61 Pearson, 1914, p. 92.

Appendix 4

1 Mary Hoban, *Footprints*, vol. 3, no. 2, October 1977.

INDEX